The Marvelous Exchange

THE MARVELOUS EXCHANGE

DISCOVERING THE POWER OF SPIRITUAL UNION WITH CHRIST

An Exposition of Romans 6:1–14

DICK FLATEN
WITH DAVID GREGORY

OPERATION 220 MINISTRIES
2017

Published by Operation 220 Ministries
formerly Exchanged Life Ministries Texas
2001 W. Plano Parkway, Suite 3800
Plano, Texas 75075
admin@operation220.org
www.operation220.org

Cover and book design by Mark McGarry
Composition by Texas Type & Book Works, Dallas, Texas

Printed in the United States of America.

*Dedicated to the faithful life of Dick Flaten,
whose single-minded devotion to Jesus Christ
shone brightly in a dark world.*

CONTENTS

Foreword

The Marvelous Exchange: Discovering the Power of Spiritual Union with Christ by Dick Flaten is a powerful book. In very clear and understandable words, Dick leads frustrated Christians out of the baffling paradox of having sin present in their lives while simultaneously wanting to live free of that entanglement. He does this by exploring Romans 6:1–14. Many have read these verses in the past without really understanding them. Dick lucidly explains the powerful truths in this passage, that in Christ we are already dead to sin and that Christ gives us the power to overcome the temptation to keep on sinning.

I believe this book will help all Christians, especially those who have been believers for many years and have felt demoralized by their continual failings to follow God's desires for their lives. As Christians begin to discover, through Dick's words, that they really can be "emancipated from the power of indwelling sin," they will find a peace in their lives that they have never had.

I strongly encourage all of those who believe in Jesus Christ to read the words Dick has written. They are written by someone who is a dear personal friend of mine, one of the men Christ has used most to influence my own life as a Christian. He has helped me as a friend, a mentor, and a pastor. I am glad he has written this book so others can experience his wonderful counsel just as I have. Remember, the words Dick writes are from the heart of a man who has lived with the threat of premature death from non-Hodgkin's lymphoma for twenty years, during which time he has undergone multiple courses of chemotherapy, radiation, and surgical procedures. Dick not only talks the talk; he also walks the walk with Christ.

JOE S. MCILHANEY, JR., M.D.
President, The Medical Institute for Sexual Health
Austin, Texas

The preceding was written in October 1997, soon after the manuscript for this book was completed. In December 1997, Dick Flaten died. Though Dick did not live to see his book in print, this great passion of his has now been realized through the help of many friends and the love of his devoted wife, Ann.

David Gregory
Dallas, Texas
May 1999

Introduction

How do we live the Christian life? How do we overcome the power of sin that still dwells within us as believers and experience the freedom that is ours in Christ? Those questions have plagued every believer for the last two thousand years. *Now that I have become a Christian, what am I supposed to do?* Or, *I have been a Christian for thirty years, and I still cannot get victory.* Are we doomed to a Christian life of mediocrity at best? Or is God's promise in Romans 8:37 ("But in all of these things (i.e., trials, sufferings) we *overwhelmingly conquer* through Him who loved us"), as well as myriad similar Scriptures, a mockery to the sincere Christian? As Paul said, "Wretched man that I am! Who will set me free . . . ?"

How do I live the life? We have all asked that. Over and over and over. Surely God has provided an answer somewhere in the New Testament. But where to look for it? My recommendation: Paul's letter to the Romans, for in Romans, writing to believers whom he had never met, Paul lays out in greatest detail the fullness of the gospel that he preached. In a nutshell, Paul says:

- Here's how to get right with God and receive God's life (chapters 1–5)
- Once you've *received* it, here's how to *experience* God's life (6–8)
- As you experience God's life, here's what it should look like (12–15)

This book assumes you have already received God's life (if not, or if you're not sure, please read Romans 3–4). I also am assuming you could use some help in experiencing God's life, because, to be honest, couldn't we all? That brings us back to where Paul addresses that issue, chapters 6–8. Again, in a nutshell, those chapters say that we experience the life of God by:

1. Knowing and counting on what happened to us at the cross of Christ. This includes what He did *for* us in His substitutionary death and what He did *in* us because of our spiritual union with Him in His death and resurrection (Romans 6:3–10).

2. Presenting ourselves unreservedly to the Person of God who now lives within us. Thus, we are enabled to depend completely on Him, not on our own self-effort, to live His resurrection life through us (Romans 6:13).

Sound uncomplicated? Actually, it is uncomplicated. What complicates matters is all of the mistaken mush that has accumulated in our minds, telling us that (1) what happened to us at the cross didn't actually happen, and that (2) we can live the

Christian life just fine through our own effort. Neither is true. That is why Paul wrote Romans 6–8, to convince the Romans that it isn't true. And that is why it is worth our while to read and study Romans 6–8, to allow God to convince us of His truth.

Although the entire three-chapter passage is worthy of careful consideration, it is beyond the scope of this book to fully consider all three chapters. What I will examine in detail is Romans 6:1–14. There, Paul directly addresses both essential points: counting on what happened to us at the cross and living in dependence on God.

If I could communicate only one section of the Bible to believers, it would be Romans 6:1–14. It most clearly states what we might call the gospel to Christians—the good news to those who have already believed. The pages that follow discuss:

- Our union with and new identity in Christ
- Our participation in the death, burial and resurrection life of Christ
- Our conflict with sin: how sin originates and how we defeat it
- Our once-for-all emancipation from the domination of the power of indwelling sin
- Our new life of dependence on Christ and His resources for Christian living

I invite you to walk with me into a deeper understanding of our union with Christ. I am convinced that this gospel to Christians, as revealed in this remarkable section of Scripture, can open exciting vistas for you! Discovering who you are in

Christ and the resources you have in Him will bring a stability, confidence and freedom that will not only surprise you; it will also *transform* you.

Overview of Romans 6:1–14

In His parables, Jesus used everyday settings of His time: farming, fishing, shepherding, wedding feasts. Given the prevalence of science fiction in our own culture (currently eight TV shows, several new movies—and who, even among non-fans, hasn't heard of Luke Skywalker and Darth Vader?), I wonder if perhaps Jesus today would not place a parable or two in a science fiction setting: "There was a certain landowner trapped in a time warp . . ."

If the Apostle Paul had written in science fiction parables, he might have used the classic 1956 film *Invasion of the Body Snatchers*. In the film, the earth is invaded by aliens in giant pea pods. Inside the pods, replicas of actual ordinary humans grow to maturity. Once fully developed, the pea-pod people replace actual people as they sleep. The people they replace cease to exist. The aliens look exactly like the humans they replace, except they live without any emotion or any capacity to experience love or joy. They are identical to humans on the outside, but inside they are devoid of true human life. The aliens have the same bodies as humans, but they are an entirely different life form. They are zombies.

A Reversed Plot

Romans 6:1–14, the good news to Christians, tells a parallel "body snatcher" story. Except this time the story is gloriously true, and God is the author, producer and director of the action.

According to the Scriptures, reality in this world is the *exact opposite* of the 1956 movie. Rather than being alive and then taken over by lifeless zombies, people are spiritually dead and only come to life when they put their trust in Christ. Their bodies are alive, their personalities are alive, but at the very core of their beings they are dead to the One who is life. They have no true life within them, though they look alive from the outside. Like the aliens in *Body Snatchers,* they are, in a very real sense, zombies—people walking around without life.

Exit Old Man, Enter New Man

So what did God do to us to make us come alive? Simply tell us to clean up our act? No! Just like in the movie, He put the old us to death. Our "old man," the independent rebel that we were by birth, was crucified with Christ. That "old man" ceased to exist. In its place God created an entirely "new man," having Christ's resurrection life. He invaded us with the *new man—the new creation! God brought about a marvelous exchange!*

As in the movie, the new man lives (temporarily) in the same body the old man used to occupy, but the person inside is new. We may not think we are new. We may not feel new. We may not even act new at times. But God says that we are new. Because we live in the same unredeemed bodies, we must still deal with sin. But at the deepest level of our being we are now new persons, new creations with new identities. The old man has passed away. The new man has come. God exchanged the old unregenerate man in Adam for the new man in Christ!

Admittedly, there is a mystery here which we will never fully understand this side of eternity. It is impossible for our minds to totally comprehend how it is that we were in Christ on the cross, that our old man was crucified with Him, that we were buried with Him, that we were raised to new life with Him, and that our "new man . . . in the likeness of God has been created in righteousness and holiness of the truth" (Ephesians 4:24). But it is true. This is the basis for Paul's teaching in Romans 6–8 about living.

The basic message of Romans 6:1–14 is this: if you are a believer in Christ, the old you is dead, the new you is alive. You are now a completely different being than before, over whom sin no longer has rule. Through living by faith, in dependence upon the Spirit within, you can experience the abundant life God has provided you.

Why This Book?

I have written this book on Romans 6:1–14 because it is the preeminent passage in all of Scripture that reveals what the "new man" is like. Although some excellent books present these truths in a topical manner, I believe there is a great need to see how the Scripture lays the foundation for this mysterious, yet marvelous truth of being a new man, a new creation in Christ. My aim is to clearly, thoroughly explain this central passage in its entirety. A person's understanding and appropriation of God's truth can get rather vague by just knowing the concept. We must be firmly anchored in this passage as it unfolds verse by verse.

As foundational and essential as these truths are to the Christian life, they are generally not understood and consequently are not appropriated by most believers. Christians basically understand that at the time of their salvation Christ's substitutionary death on the cross accomplished their forgiveness and reconciliation with God—the past tense of the gospel. But most have never grasped all that was provided for them in their spiritual union with Christ on the cross and His consequent resurrection—the heart of the present tense of the gospel. The present tense of the gospel is one of the church's best kept secrets.

Paul's epistle to the Romans presents the gospel more thoroughly and clearly than any other part of Scripture. In chapters 3–8 he explains that there are three parts to the good news. The following overview outlines the good news which those chapters present.

The Gospel of the Grace of God

1. Delivered from the *penalty* of sin (Romans 3–5). God did something *for* the believer in Christ's substitutionary death on the cross by judicially *declaring* or *crediting* him with His perfect righteousness on the basis of faith alone. This deliverance is *past tense,* something that is already accomplished. It is what the Bible calls "justification."

2. Delivered from the control of the *power* of sin (Romans 6–8). God did something radical *to* and *in* the believer by placing him or her, at the moment of conversion, into union with Christ in His death, burial, and resurrection. The believer has become a new creation, a new person, having Christ's perfectly righteous life imparted to him or her. This righteousness is both *past tense*—something that has already been imparted to the believer—and *present*

tense—something that is being progressively accomplished in the believer as, day by day, the Christian is being gradually conformed to the image of Christ. This is what the Bible calls "sanctification."

3. Delivered from the *presence* of sin (Romans 8). One day, God will fully and finally conform us to His image and give us a resurrection body. This righteousness is *future tense,* and is a completed or perfect righteousness—what the Bible calls "glorification."

As we lay hold of the entirety of the gospel, we will be able to deal effectively with the *cause* of our problems and not simply the *symptoms.* We will be able to experience the abundant life that Jesus promised, but which seems to elude so many believers.

PART ONE

THE EXCHANGE ACCOMPLISHED

CHAPTER ONE

YOUR INCALCULABLE WEALTH

What shall we say then? Are we to continue in sin that grace may increase? May it never be! How shall we who died to sin still live in it? ROMANS 6:1,2

BILL BRIGHT, founder and president of Campus Crusade for Christ, has a favorite true story he loves to tell. Years ago, while visiting his brother in West Texas, Bill learned of Ira Yates, a sheep rancher in the area. In the 1930s, during the Great Depression, Mr. Yates was living at a subsistence level. His sheep ranching operation was not making money. He was mortgaged to the hilt to the bank, unable to make payments, and in danger of losing the ranch. As with so many people of that time, he was living on a government subsidy for the bare necessities of life for himself and his family.

One day a seismographic crew came into the area representing an oil company. They said, "According to our calculations, Mr. Yates, there is a possibility that there is oil on your land." They persuaded him to sign a lease to drill a wildcat test

well. The company began to drill . . . 800 . . . 900 . . . 1,000 feet
. . . 1,100 feet. At 1,115 feet they struck oil. It was the largest
known oil strike in America at that time, with a daily yield of
80,000 barrels—worth over one million a day in today's dol-
lars! Yet that was just the beginning. Many more wells followed, some twice as productive as the first. After the oil had
pumped for more than thirty years, a test of just one of the
wells showed that it still had a potential flow of 125,000 barrels a day. The one-time sheep rancher, Ira Yates, owned it all.
Previously, he had worried about paying his bills. All the time
he was walking over a mammoth underground lake of oil. He
was living as if impoverished, yet he was a multimillionaire.
What was the problem? He didn't know the wealth that was
right beneath his feet.

This in a very real sense illustrates the incalculable wealth
you and I have in our union with Jesus Christ. At the moment
of new birth we have this wealth to draw upon, instead of living in spiritual poverty. But if it is to be a reality in our lives,
we must *tap into,* or *appropriate,* this supernatural life that is
ours in Christ.

What is this wealth that we have in Christ, and how do we
draw upon it? To answer that, we will study verses 1 and 2 of
Romans 6, verses which lay the foundation for the Apostle
Paul's teaching in this chapter. First, however, let us take a
brief look at the preceding passage, Romans 5:12–21, which
establishes a context for Romans 6.

Context

The primary purpose of Romans 5:12–21 is to present con-
cisely the good news of the riches that are now ours in Christ.

Upon reading this passage you may think it is chiefly concerned with bad news (our connection to Adam) rather than with our connection as believers to Christ. We are seen by birth to be united with Adam in the fall of mankind. Yet the main focus of the passage is not Adam but the "much more" that we have in Christ. Adam serves as a *contrast* to Christ. For us to grasp all that we have in Christ we must understand all that we were in Adam. Verses 12–14 say:

> Nevertheless death reigned from Adam until Moses, even over those who had not sinned in the likeness of the offense of Adam, who is a type of Him who was to come. But the free gift is not like the transgression. For if by the transgression of the one the many died, much more did the grace of God and the gift by the grace of the one Man, Jesus Christ, abound to the many. And the gift is not like that which came through the one who sinned; for on the one hand the judgment arose from one transgression resulting in condemnation, but on the other hand the free gift arose from many transgressions resulting in justification.

Adam and Christ are similar in that each is the representative head of his respective group of humanity. Bob Smith explained in *From Guilt to Glory:*

> Adam was the beginning of the *first creation,* and the result of his action in the fall brought with it certain consequences for his whole race. Similarly Christ is the beginning of a *new creation,* and the result of His action in redemption brought certain consequences also. The contrast is in the consequences. In Adam they were all negative—and deadly. In Christ they are all positive—and *life-giving.* And throughout the passage the emphasis is *much more, more than that, all the more,* telling us that Christ's redemptive act on the cross *more* than overcame the effects of Adam's sin.[1]

Our union with Adam, which began at the moment of our natural birth, resulted in our being "made sinners" (5:19). We were under the reign of sin and death, utterly condemned. By contrast, our union with Christ, which began at the moment of our spiritual birth, resulted in our being "made righteous" (5:19). As John MacArthur says:

> Adam's *disobedience* caused him and his descendants to be *made sinners* by nature and constitution. In the same way, but with the exact opposite effect, Christ's *obedience* causes those who believe in Him to be *made righteous* by nature and constitution.[2]

David Needham amplifies this amazing truth:

> Contrary to much popular teaching, regeneration (being born again), is more than having something taken away (sins forgiven) or having something added to you (a new nature with the assistance of the Holy Spirit); it is becoming something you had never been before. This new identity is not on the flesh level, but the spirit level—one's deepest self. This miracle is more than a "judicial" act of God. It is an act so REAL that it is right to say that a Christian's essential nature is righteous rather than sinful. All other lesser identities each of us has can only be understood and appreciated by our acceptance of and response to this fact.[3]

As genuine believers we not only have been judicially declared righteous on the basis of faith alone (justification), but we have had Christ's perfectly righteous and dynamic life imparted within, through our union with Him (sanctification). We have become entirely new persons, new creations at the very core of our being. Our essential identity is now that of those who are experientially righteous because of their vital union with Christ. We are no longer primarily unworthy sinners before a holy God, but righteous saints who still do sin.

The Logical Objection

Having described in Romans 1–5 the marvelous truth of justification by grace through faith alone, our consequent assurance of salvation in Christ, and the riches of our union with Christ, Paul concludes this section by exclaiming: "And the Law came in that the transgression might increase; but where sin increased, grace abounded all the more, that, as sin reigned in death, even so grace might reign through righteousness to eternal life through Jesus Christ our Lord" (Romans 5:20–21).

Anticipating an objection to what has been presented thus far and especially to 5:20–21, Paul begins chapter 6 by asking, *"What shall we say then? Are we to continue in sin that grace might increase?"*

If we do not understand the grace of God, believing we must perform to obtain God's acceptance, we may understandably raise this objection. We may consider Paul's teaching a casting aside of all moral restraint, issuing a license to sin. We may rationalize:

> If I have been justified freely by the grace of God, and am therefore saved by faith alone in Christ and His substitutionary death for me, then I can live as I please. If I sin, I know that I will be forgiven. In fact, God will have a greater opportunity to demonstrate His grace when I sin.

Paul, through the inspiration of the Holy Spirit, understood the implications of the objector's mindset. Following this way of thinking, people would rationalize that it is acceptable to *"continue in sin."* But in verse 2 the apostle states that, to anyone who understands what happened to believers at the cross, this conclusion is *outrageous!*

Our Death to Sin

"May it never be! How shall we who died to sin still live in it?" The possibility of continuing in sin elicits the strongest possible negative response in the Greek text: *"May it never be!"* The King James Version actually translates it, *"God forbid!"* The idea of a Christian living a lifestyle of sin is *repugnant* to the apostle. Why? Because something profoundly, radically, permanently transforming has happened to us in Christ. We *"died to sin!"*

John Murray rightly calls Romans 6:2 the "fundamental premise" of the apostle's thought in this chapter. This fundamental premise of our having died to sin is repeated directly in *every* verse from verses 3 through 8, and indirectly in verses 9 and 10. Because we are in union with Christ, everything that happened to Him has happened to us. In verse 11, Paul makes application of our death to sin (as well as our resurrection with Christ): *"Even so consider yourselves to be dead to sin, but alive to God in Christ Jesus."* This application continues in verses 12 through 14.

It is important for us to understand that the verb "died" is expressed in the Greek aorist tense, which here refers to a single action that has occurred in the past. Thus, "died" does not mean that "we are dying to sin" (present tense), nor "we shall die to sin" (future tense). "Died" means a past action. A death *has already* occurred.

Past action

8

The statement, "we *died to sin,*" is crucial to our understanding both of the passage and how to experience the joy of supernatural living. It is the fundamental basis by which God gives us power over indwelling sin. James Boice said,

> To understand this statement is to understand how to live a holy life. And *because* it is the key to sanctification, I would go so far as to say that Romans 6:2 is the most important verse in the Bible for believers in evangelical churches to understand today.[4]

What does it mean that we died to sin? Let us first consider what it does *not* mean.

Three Wrong Views of "Dead to Sin"

1.   The Christian Is No Longer Responsive to Sin

This view is an argument from analogy. A dead body has no senses that function. It can no longer respond to stimuli because its senses are dead to them. If a body is lying motionless, it is easy to see whether it is alive by throwing a bucket of cold water in the face. If the body is dead, it will not respond to this or any other stimulus.

The logical application of this view is that one who died to sin is unresponsive to it. When temptation comes he is immune, insensitive to the appeal and power of sin. Verses 11–13 of this chapter, plus the rest of Scripture, easily refute this view. And simple honesty with ourselves refutes such thinking convincingly. Christians are simply not immune to the lure of sin. Therefore, being dead to sin cannot mean that we do not respond to its stimuli.

2. The Christian Should Die to Sin

Some hold that Christians *should* die to sin because sin is still active in their lives when they come to saving faith in Christ. According to this view, when a person becomes a believer, he is urged to resist the desire to sin and so die to sin's power.

To the question, "Have you died to sin?" the believer with this view might say, "I surely would like to die to sin" or "I am trying to die to sin" or "How do you do that?" or "I just don't *feel* dead to sin; therefore I must not be dead to sin."

Neil Anderson relates the following:

> A pastor stopped by my office one day and said, "I have been struggling for 22 years in my Christian experience. It's been one trial after another, and I think I know what my problem is. I was doing my devotions the other day when I came across Colossians 3:3, 'For you have died, and your life is now hidden with Christ in God.' That's the key to victory, isn't it?" I assured him I agreed. Then he asked, "How do I do that?"
>
> I was surprised by his question, so I asked him to look at the passage again and read it just a little slower. So he read it again, "For you died, and your life is hidden with Christ in God." Again he asked in desperation, "I know I need to die with Christ, but how do I do it?" This dear man has been desperately trying for 22 years to do something that has already been done, to become someone he already is. He's not alone. Many Bible-believing Christians are bogged down [regarding] maturity and victory because they are trying to become something they already are.[5]

The apostle is not telling us that we *should* die to sin. Rather he is telling us that we *already* died to sin. The past tense is used throughout verses 2–10. This is not something we do. It is something that has already been done to us permanently, what God did to us in the death of His Son. Because of what has happened to us, we are now no longer obligated to continue in sin.

The believer does not die to sin day by day. He has already died to sin once for all because of his union with Christ in His death (Romans 6:3–4). But he needs to *apply* this already accomplished death to sin to his everyday experience. In Romans 6:12–13 the apostle explains how to make operative this death to the power of sin. These verses will be examined in detail in Chapter 5.

3. The Christian's Death to Sin's Guilt and Condemnation Frees Him from the Power of Sin

Another wrong view is the belief that deliverance from the penalty of sin is all that is necessary to effect our death to sin. Christ's substitutionary death *for us* is portrayed as a vague cure-all to our sin problem. As foundational and essential as deliverance from sin's guilt and condemnation are, our Lord's death on the cross accomplished much more than that!

Christ's death for us did, indeed, free us from the condemnation and guilt of sin. But we can be forgiven and still be defeated by sin's power. To deliver us from the control of the power of sin, God had to do more than just free us from its guilt and condemnation.

God did something intrinsic and vital *to us* and *in us* by placing us into spiritual union with Christ in His death, burial and resurrection. As we will see in the next chapter, this union is the basis of our having died to sin, resulting in our deliverance from the dominion of sin.

What Does it Mean to Be Dead to Sin?

Being dead to sin means that we who have experienced new birth in Christ are no longer in bondage to the control of sin in our lives. It is not that we cannot sin. We can and do sin, but our union with Christ has given us the ability not to *have to sin* any longer. James Boice recalls how Augustine described the believer's state with regard to sin:

> Augustine said that before he fell Adam was *posse pecarre* ("able to sin"). He had not sinned yet, but he was able to. After his fall, according to Augustine, Adam became *non posse non peccare* ("not able not to sin"). By himself he was unable to break free from it. The state of believers . . . is now one of *posse non peccare* ("able not to sin"). That is the state Paul is writing about in Romans 6. For them, the tyranny of sin has been broken.[6]

This truth is absolutely revolutionary for the believer! An analogy by Larry Christenson illuminates what has resulted in our lives.

> Think of yourself as living in an apartment house . . . under a landlord who has made your life miserable. He charges you exorbitant rent. When you can't pay, he loans you money at a fearful rate of interest . . . He barges into your apartment at all hours of the day and night, wrecks and dirties up the place, then charges you extra for not maintaining the premises. Your life is miserable. Then comes Someone who says, "I've taken over this apartment house. I've purchased it. You can live here as long as you like, free. The rent is paid up. I am going to be living here with you, in the manager's apartment." What a joy! You are saved! You are delivered out of the clutches of the old landlord!
>
> But what happens? You hardly have time to rejoice in your

newfound freedom, when a knock comes at the door. And there he is—the old landlord! Mean, glowering, and demanding as ever. He has come for the rent, he says.

What do you do? Do you pay him? Of course, you don't! Do you go out and pop him on the nose? No—he's bigger than you are! You confidently tell him, "You'll have to take that up with the new Landlord." He may bellow, threaten, wheedle, and cajole. You just quietly tell him, "Take it up with the new Landlord." If he comes back a dozen times, with all sorts of threats and arguments, waving legal-looking documents in your face, you simply tell him yet once again, "Take it up with the new Landlord." In the end he has to. He knows it, too. He just hopes that he can bluff and threaten and deceive you into doubting the new Landlord will really take care of things.

Now this is the situation of a Christian. Once Christ has delivered you from the power of sin and the devil, you can depend on it: that old landlord will soon come back knocking at your door. And what is your defense? . . . You send him to the new Landlord. *You send him to Jesus.*[7]

Although this illustration does not fully express what has happened to us in our death to sin, it beautifully conveys the *result:* we do not *have* to sin any longer. We will have to wait until we get to verses 3–7 to understand the full implications of this liberating truth. God caused an *intrinsic change* to take place within us because of our spiritual union with Christ in His death, burial and resurrection. Taking Christenson's excellent illustration further, consider the following: portray the "old us" (the tenant dominated by the previous landlord) as having been put to death, and the "new us" (the tenant under the new landlord) as now raised from the dead. This addition to the illustration reveals the *basis* of our deliverance from the reign of sin. Because we died in Christ's death and were made alive in His resurrection, we are dead to sin.

The "old landlord" is the power of indwelling sin. It still resides within us after our spiritual new birth, but it has been stripped of its authority!

Should we continue in sin that grace might increase? No way! Why? Because we died to sin. As we will clearly see in the next chapter, the reason we died to sin is because God placed us into permanent union with Christ in His death, burial, and resurrection. We are now a new creation in Christ, a new creation over whom sin has no claim or control!

We can and must tap into God's inexhaustible resources of spiritual wealth and freedom. We no longer have to live in the oppression of spiritual poverty and bondage, just as sheep rancher Ira Yates no longer had to live in material poverty and bondage when he discovered the vast riches he actually possessed.

As mentioned at the start of this chapter, verses 1 and 2 lay the foundation for the rest of the apostle's teaching in Romans 6. Paul will continue to unfold for us verse by verse the incalculable riches that our glorious God has provided for us in our union with Christ.

Summary Paraphrase of Verses 1–2

How should we respond to this tremendous grace of God? Should we just go on sinning, so that God has an opportunity to show more and more of His grace? Absolutely not! That is preposterous! If that is your response, you have completely missed the truth of what God did to you and in you at the cross. You have died to sin. It no longer has control over you. How could you possibly still live that old, miserable way? You have already been freed from it.

PART TWO

KNOWING THE EXCHANGE WAS MADE

CHAPTER TWO

WHO AM I?

"Or do you not know that all of us who have been baptized into Christ Jesus have been baptized into His death? Therefore we have been buried with Him through baptism into death, in order that as Christ was raised from the dead through the glory of the Father, so we too might walk in newness of life. For if we have become united with Him in the likeness of His death, certainly we shall be also in the likeness of His resurrection." ROMANS 6:3–5

WHO AM I? That question has echoed in the hearts of man throughout the ages, in every generation.

"I'm a business person."

"I'm a teacher."

"I'm a mother."

"I'm a husband."

"I'm an American."

"I'm a Christian."

We draw our identity from many sources. As Christians, it is easy to overlook our one true identity in Christ.

Maxwell Maltz, author of *Psycho-Cybernetics,* discovered as a plastic surgeon that a patient's deep-seated self-image consistently determined his or her attitudes and actions. He wrote: "A human being always acts and feels and performs in accordance with what he imagines to be true about himself."[1]

Dr. Maltz described many cases where plastic surgery dramatically changed the personalities of his patients, and conversely, how others received new faces and yet remained their same old selves.

In one case, a couple brought their daughter to a plastic surgeon because of her unusually large nose. She was shy and withdrawn, having a deep sense of inferiority. She felt ugly in comparison to her very attractive, outgoing family. The plastic surgery on her nose was more than successful. When the bandages were removed the doctor marveled at how beautiful the girl was. When he held the mirror to her face, however, her eyes got progressively sadder and she finally burst into tears. To her, the surgery was a failure and she still looked the same.

No one was able to persuade her that she was now beautiful. Because her self-image of being unattractive was so deeply imbedded within, she could not see the transformation that had so obviously taken place. Only after meeting with a psychologist for six months did she believe she really had become beautiful. Her personality quickly underwent a dramatic change. She became warm, outgoing and enthusiastic. She now began to act and feel in accordance with what she believed herself to be.

The skill of a plastic surgeon is amazing, but it cannot compare with the profound and radical transformation that takes place the moment we are born spiritually through faith in Christ. "Therefore if any man is in Christ, he is a new creature;

the old things passed away; behold, new things have come" (2 Corinthians 5:17). This verse does not say that we *will become* new creations. We already are new creations. We have been created a new person, with a new life and a new identity. God wants us to believe and act in accordance with what we now are.

In Romans 6:3–5, we see *how* God has made us new creations in Christ: by placing us into spiritual union with Him in his death, burial and resurrection. How very revolutionary and practical is this truth if only we believe and appropriate it in our daily lives!

We saw in Chapter 1 of this book how Paul dealt with a potential objection, *"Are we to continue in sin that grace might increase?"* He answered with the most emphatic words possible in verse 2: *"May it never be! How shall we who died to sin still live in it?"*

We looked at various wrong ways of interpreting our death to sin: (1) that believers are immune to sin; (2) that the believer *should* die to sin; and (3) that the believer has died to sin's guilt and condemnation only. In contrast to these misinterpretations, we said that being dead to sin means that the authority or rule of sin has been broken in the believer's life once for all. We are now free *not* to sin. In other words, we don't *have* to sin anymore.

How did God bring about our death to sin?

Two Key Words

In verses 3–5 we encounter two words that help unlock the meaning of our spiritual union with Christ: "baptized" and "united."

Baptized

Paul asks, *"Or do you not know that all of us who have been baptized into Christ Jesus have been baptized into His death?"*

"Baptized" is a transliteration (not a translation) of the Greek word *baptizo*. That is, rather than translate the Greek into the English words having the same meaning, the translators created an English word out of the Greek word. *Baptizo* literally means "to place into." Metaphorically it means "to change the identity of something or someone."

In the New Testament, *baptizo* is used in two major ways—water baptism and Spirit baptism. Spirit baptism is the act of the Holy Spirit placing the believer into spiritual union with Christ, including union in His death, burial and resurrection.[2] Water baptism is the outward sign used to indicate that a person has died, been buried, and been raised with Christ. As the Westminster Confession of Faith states: "Baptism is an outward, visible symbol of an inward, spiritual reality."

In the New Testament, Spirit baptism and water baptism were closely associated, usually occurring almost simultaneously. When a person placed his faith in Christ (and thus was Spirit baptized), he was water baptized as soon as possible, as a witness to his new found faith. While water baptism is not the focus in Romans 6, baptism by immersion does best symbolize the spiritual reality that Paul describes.

New Testament scholar Kenneth Wuest defines baptism as "placing a person or a thing into a new environment or into union with something else so as to alter its condition or its relationship to its previous environment or condition." Of Romans 6:3–4 he says:

> The believing sinner is introduced or placed into Christ, thus coming into union with Him. By that action he is taken out of

his old environment and condition in which he had lived, the First Adam, and is placed into a new environment and condition, the Last Adam.[3]

We were placed into Christ and therefore into spiritual union with Him. We were taken out of our old environment in Adam where we were under the law of sin and death and placed into our new environment in Christ, where we have righteousness and life.

Spirit baptism is the invisible spiritual operation that places the believing sinner into union with the Savior in His death. Thus, when Christ died, we died with Him. Not only does Paul say we died with Christ, he also says that we were "buried" with Him (verse 4). Nothing could be more final and conclusive in death than to be buried. Because of our union with Christ in His death and burial, at the very core of our being the old person that we were before salvation died and was buried. (We will see this more clearly in our next chapter when we examine Romans 6:6. It is sufficient to say at this point that our old person or "old man," who was preeminently characterized by an independent, rebellious heart, literally was put to death and buried because of being placed into Christ in His death and burial.)

But that is not all. We are now partakers with Christ in His *resurrection!* The ultimate purpose of our death and burial with Christ is stated in verse 4: *"in order that as Christ was raised from the dead through the glory of the Father, so we too might walk in newness of life."*

Awesome, isn't it? If you're a believer in Christ you have undergone a marvelous transformation by being baptized (placed) into Christ in His death, burial and resurrection. We are now literally—not figuratively—partakers of Christ's resurrection! What a profound change has taken place in the believer's life![4]

United

The second word that helps unlock the meaning of our new identity and being dead to sin is "united." *"For if we have become united with Him in the likeness of His death, certainly we shall be also in the likeness of His resurrection"* (verse 5). ("Likeness" means that what happened to Christ physically happened to us spiritually.)

"United" literally means "to grow together," conveying an intimate union. Christ illustrated this union between Himself and the believer when He said in John 15:5: "I am the vine and you are the branches." The vine (Christ) and the branches (us) are in *spiritual union* with each other and share a common life.[5] We have been baptized (placed) into Christ so that we are now in union with Him. Numerous writers on Romans confirm how absolutely vital this truth is.

John Murray:

Union with Christ is the central truth of the whole doctrine of salvation.[6]

Arthur W. Pink:

The subject of spiritual union is the most important, most profound, and yet the most blessed of any that is set forth in the sacred Scriptures; and yet, sad to say, there is hardly any which is now more generally neglected. The very expression "spiritual union" is unknown in most professing Christian circles, and even where it is employed it is given such a protracted meaning as to take in only a fragment of this precious truth. Probably its very profundity is the reason why it is so largely ignored.[7]

James M. Boice:

What has the Holy Spirit done for our salvation? He has joined us to Christ, so that we become the beneficiaries of all Christ has done. . . . . It is terribly important and perhaps the most critical doctrine of salvation in Paul's writing. Paul used the phrases "in Christ," "in Christ Jesus," "in Him," or their equivalents, 164 times in his writings. We can hardly emphasize this enough.[8]

Let's make sure we understand this revolutionary truth by considering a few questions:

- If you are in Christ, where were you when Christ died on the cross?
- What happened to you there?
- After Christ was crucified, what happened to Him? What happened to you?
- When He was raised from the dead, what happened to you?

If you and I are in Christ, then we died when Christ died. We were buried when He was buried. And in Him, we are risen. Who are we now? What is our essential identity? We are new creatures in Christ! And the result is that we are free not to sin. Why did God arrange for your death and mine? So He could exchange our old life in Adam for Christ's life in us— the marvelous exchange!

At this point it is vital that you understand that you have been joined to One who is eternal. Christ is not time-dimensional. He sees the past, present and future simultaneously; they are all the same to God. Everything is present tense with Him. Consequently, what happened to you when you were placed into Him is not time-dimensional; it is timeless. This union is so real, so vital, so complete and so trans-historical that when Christ died, you died, too. When He was buried, you were buried. When He was raised, you were raised. [9]

Recently I was asked by a friend, "I know the Scriptures teach that we are in spiritual union with Christ, but I really don't understand this. Could you help make sense of it for me?" I acknowledged that this truth seems to be abstract, nebulous and therefore confusing. I emphasized that it is the Holy Spirit who ultimately must make the truth real to us (Ephesians 1:18–21). I went on to give him an illustration of these truths that has been most helpful to me personally. I call it "the divine surgery."

At your natural birth, you were in Adam (Romans 5:12–19). Let's imagine yourself a hand attached to the wrist of Adam. As a hand you were capable of human good and human evil, but even the human good that you could do fell woefully short of God's standard of perfection. Actually, as a hand of Adam, you were joined to a source of life that God has rejected. That which flowed through your veins was under the law of sin and death and was characterized by self-centeredness, independence and rebellion toward God and His will.

But at your spiritual birth, divine surgery took place; you, the hand of Adam, were transplanted and grafted onto the wrist of Christ. A marvelous exchange took place. You are now vitally and permanently joined to Christ, your new Head, the Head of the body, which is the church (Ephesians 5:23). The same life that is in the Head courses through you, the hand; it is Christ's very life that you share. Also, in this new union with Christ, you took on the *past experience, the past history* of the One you have been vitally joined to. Specifically, the Scripture tells us that we were joined to Christ in His death, burial and resurrection.

Remembering that the eternal Christ is not time-dimensional and that everything is present tense with Him, picture yourself as a hand of our Lord's body as He hung on the cross nearly two thousand years ago. Just as He was crucified on that cross, so also were you as His hand. Next, view yourself as a hand in His body as He lay dead in the burial tomb. And finally, see yourself as His hand as He rose bodily from the grave—and as you are presently joined spiritually to Him in His resurrection life. This illustration, of course, has its limitations, but in a very real sense it portrays our union with Him:

When Christ died, you died
When Christ was buried, you were buried
When Christ was raised, you were raised

The old you (the old man in Adam) was executed in Christ's death and has been replaced by the new you (the new man in Christ), who has been created in Christ's resurrection. And this new creation is now who you really are at the deepest level of your being.

In order for this truth to be more than a cognitive understanding, and instead become a spiritual reality in your heart, I would urge you to take time to *meditate* on this illustration in the light of Romans 6. In fact, memorizing the passage and using it devotionally, along with an illustration like this, will greatly aid the Holy Spirit in making all of this a reality in your life intellectually, volitionally and emotionally. This process certainly works for me.

Another simple illustration can help us understand being baptized into Christ (verse 3) and being united with Him (verse 5). Place a sheet of paper within a book. The paper represents you; the book represents Christ. At our new birth, we are placed into Christ, just as the paper is placed into the book. Whatever happens to the book happens to the paper. Ship the book to a distant location and the paper goes with it. Drop the book and the paper drops with it. Raise the book up and the paper is raised up also. In the same way, we are now inextricably bound and identified with the Lord Jesus Christ in His death, burial and resurrection. *What happened to Him happened to us.*

As we try to understand these two phenomena of being baptized into Christ and being united with Him, perhaps you are still wondering, "How do I do that?" The answer is that you *cannot.* It has already been done for you the moment you placed your faith in Christ as your Savior and Lord. The challenge before us now is: will we believe and appropriate what God has already done for us in Christ by placing us in His death, burial and resurrection?

Personalizing the Truth

The fact that we have been placed into Christ, united with Him in His death, burial and resurrection, and that we have a new identity in Him, has enormous implications for our daily lives. For example, even after they are saved most believers continue to struggle with feeling that they have to perform to be acceptable to God. We call this performance-based acceptance. We initially had to abandon our attempts to gain such acceptance with God when we came to Him for salvation. We came by faith alone with no merit—no performance—on our part. But inevitably we as believers seem to fall back into the same trap of performance-based acceptance with others, with ourselves and with God.

I've experienced this trap. After being a committed Christian for twenty-five years and a pastor for fifteen, this issue surfaced dramatically in my life, even though I understood and was consistently appropriating such truths as:

- The spiritual battle is either won or lost in our thought life
- The Christian life is a walk of dependence upon Christ rather than relying upon our own resources
- The power of sin has been broken in the believer's life through Christ's death, burial and resurrection. We now have the ability not to sin.

While I was pastoring a flourishing church and consistently teaching these truths, I developed a strain in my throat muscles. Thinking I was misusing my voice, I went to the University of Texas in Austin for speech therapy. When asked whether the strain might be stress related, I confidently stated that stress was not a significant problem for me because of my reliance upon the Lord. We proceeded with the therapy. I was taught various exercises to relax the throat muscles, as well as how to identify the correct pitch for my voice. But the strain in my throat persisted.

Finally I met personally with the professor who had been

following my case. She did not believe that I was misusing my voice, but suggested that my problem was stress induced. Then she added, "Mr. Flaten, have you thought about getting counseling?" I was taken aback by her question, seeing myself more in the role of a counselor than a counselee. Embarrassed, I agreed that I probably needed help in time management. However, in the months that followed I did not consider the throat problem serious enough to pursue counseling. Shortly thereafter, I received the devastating news that I had non-Hodgkin's lymphoma in various areas of my body. I began chemotherapy and radiation treatments.

The speech therapy professor had not gotten my attention, but the cancer had! I became convinced that stress had significantly contributed to my condition. The question was: what was causing the stress? Some insights came quickly, but it took some time before the Lord revealed the most basic cause. I was in many ways still caught up in a *performance-based self-acceptance,* despite understanding and appropriating the grace of God in so many other ways.

Somehow, subtly and unconsciously, I thought that if I performed well enough (especially in my ministry) I would gain what I longed for—a sense of significance, acceptance, and love from other people, from myself, and even, in a certain sense, from God.

Often I did not feel satisfied with my performance. A voice within seemed to demand, "More! Perform more! Then you will be accepted!" When I had "blown it," I was assaulted with self-condemning thoughts like, "You're such a loser," or "What's the use?" I was allowing my performance to dictate my sense of self-acceptance.

I have found that I was not alone in seeking acceptance

through performance. Many others have told me it is true of them as well. This bondage operates in concert through the mind, will, and emotions.

1. WITH OUR MIND: we *believe* we must perform for acceptance from ourselves and others. (We *believe* we are inadequate.)
2. WITH OUR WILL: we *choose* to perform for acceptance. (We *act* according to our sense of inadequacy.)
3. WITH OUR EMOTIONS: we *feel* worthy of acceptance only when we perform well. (We *feel* inadequate.)

All of us need love, acceptance, and a sense of significance. God created us with these needs. But He never intended for performance on our part to be the *means* of satisfying these needs.

The Basis for Acceptance

What is God's solution to the awful bondage of performance-based self-acceptance? His unconditional acceptance (and love) of us in Christ. When we truly grasp what God has done for us in Christ and who we now are in Him, we will be able to more fully experience God's unconditional acceptance and love toward us. We no longer depend on our performance to meet our need for acceptance.

We are forgiven, new creations with a new identity. Just as the young woman in the introduction of this chapter experienced a dramatic personality change when she underwent plastic surgery on her nose, we will experience a transformation spiritually that staggers the imagination when we accept ourselves in accordance with our new identity.

Some mistakenly think that having a new identity in Christ is like being a participant in the FBI's Witness Protection Program. Agreeing to testify against a dangerous criminal, participants are moved to a new city and given a new identity: a new name, new ID cards, a new personal history, and so forth. They are, in fact, the same person, but their outward identity has been changed to ensure their safety. In the same way, some Christians reason, they have been given a new outward identity by God. To them, they are still the same person as before, but because they are "in Christ," God says that they have a new identity.

But that is not at all what the Scriptures teach. As we will see more clearly in the next chapter, the Scriptures teach that we have a new identity, because we are, in fact, new persons. Because we have been united with Christ in His death, burial and resurrection, the person we used to be no longer exists. God has not simply slapped a new identity onto the same old person. We have *actually* been miraculously changed through our union with Christ. (Supernaturally)

As a result, when thoughts such as "I am unacceptable" or "I am such a worthless sinner" begin to assail us, we must consciously, deliberately refuse to accept our old identity that was programmed into our minds and instead rest in our new identity that has already been imparted to us in Christ's death, burial and resurrection. We need to appropriate the *literalness* of our new creation in Christ. Once we understand and apply the truth of who we really are, it is relatively easy for the true child of God to say, "My performance is not the measure of who I am."

At the moment of our new birth we became perfectly significant and accepted in Christ. God executed the old man in Adam (our old identity) and replaced him with the new man in Christ (our new identity). No amount of performance on our part will improve upon what He has done for us in Christ.

We will see even more clearly in the next chapter that the old "you" before salvation (your previous identity) was executed in Christ's death and now has been *replaced* by the new "you" (your new identity) who has been created in Christ's resurrection.

Summary Paraphrase of Verses 3-5

Don't you realize that you have been placed into spiritual union with Christ? That is how God brought about your death to sin. The old you was under the domination of sin. But when Christ died on the cross, you died with Him. When He was buried, you were buried with Him. When He was resurrected, you were resurrected with Him. This means that whereas once you were partakers of Adam and the sin and death that he brought, now you are partakers of Christ's resurrected life. That is your new identity. You are perfectly accepted in that new identity. And you are able to live an overcoming life through His resurrected life in you.

CHAPTER THREE

YOUR FREEDOM BREAKTHROUGH

"Knowing this, that our old self was crucified with Him, that our body of sin might be done away with, that we should no longer be slaves to sin; for he who has died is freed from sin." ROMANS 6: 6, 7

THE THIRTEENTH AMENDMENT to the Constitution abolished slavery in the United States. President Lincoln said of it: "I congratulate myself, this country, and the whole world on this great moral victory." It was indeed a great moral victory, but that "victory" meant little to many in the South. As Charles Swindoll has commented:

> Something happened that many would have never expected. The vast majority of slaves in the South who were legally freed continued to live on as slaves. Most of them went right on living as though nothing had happened. Though free, the blacks lived virtually unchanged lives throughout the Reconstruction Period.

I call that tragic. A war had been fought. A president had been assassinated. An amendment to the Constitution had now been signed into law. Once-enslaved men, women, and children were now legally emancipated. Yet amazingly, many continued to live in fear and squalor. In a context of hard-earned freedom, slaves chose to remain as slaves. Cruel and brutal though many of their owners were, black men and women chose to keep on serving the same old masters until they died. There were a few brave exceptions but in many parts of the country you'd never have known that slavery had been officially abolished and that they had been emancipated. That's the way the plantation owners wanted it. They maintained the age-old philosophy, "Keep 'em ignorant and you keep 'em in the field."

Now if you think that is tragic, I can tell you one far worse. It has to do with Christians living today as slaves. Even though our Great Emancipator, Christ the Lord, paid the ultimate price to overthrow slavery once for all, most Christians act as though they're still held in bondage. In fact, strange as it is, most seem to prefer the security of slavery to the risks of liberty. And our slave master, Satan, loves it so. He is delighted that so many have bought into that lie and live under the dark shadow of such ignorance. He sits like the proverbial fat cat, grinning, "Great! Go right on livin' like a slave!" even though he knows we have been liberated from his control. More than most in God's family, the adversary knows we are free, but he hates it. So he does everything in his power to keep us pinned down in shame, guilt, ignorance, and intimidation.[1]

How about you? Are you still living in bondage to sin—even though God has set us free?

Thus far we have seen the astounding truth that we died to sin (Romans 6:2). Sin's control over the believer has been broken so that we are now free *not* to sin! In verses 3–5 we saw the unique means that God used to bring about our death to sin: He placed us into spiritual union with Christ in His death, burial and resurrection. We now have a new identity and resources as new creatures in Christ, free to fully participate in His resurrection life.

In this chapter we will encounter truth that is even more specific concerning our spiritual union with Christ. The God who made us knew how to fix what was wrong with us. As we examine this chapter I am confident that His Spirit can guide us into a clearer understanding of what He has done for us in Christ at the cross.

Three Consequences of Our Union with Christ

Verses 6 and 7 give three consequences of the Christian's union with Christ. They are sequential, with one leading to the next, and all culminating in the last consequence:

1. The original source of sin in us—our "old self" or "old man"—has ceased to exist. It has been dealt a permanent death blow.
2. Because our old man or old self is dead, the still existing "body of sin" (the vehicle of indwelling sin) has been stripped of its authority and dominance over us.
3. Consequently, we are freed from slavery to sin.

1. The Old Man Was Crucified with Christ

The first consequence of our union with Christ is the death of our "old self": *"knowing this, that our old self was crucified with Him"* (v. 6a).

This term "old self" as it is rendered here in the New American Standard Bible (NASB) is literally "old man" in the Greek. (It is preferable to use the literal term because the word "self" has so many different uses today.) Who then is this "old man" that was crucified with Christ? There is a consensus among Bible scholars that this term refers to our old unregenerate person before salvation, what we inherited from Adam—a sinner who had the heart of a rebel and was under the bondage of sin and death. The preceding context of Romans 5:12–21 supports this view. The old man was the person I used to be and no longer am. God executed this old unregenerate man in Christ's death, resurrecting in his place the "new man" (Ephesians 4:24). This truth is of the very highest importance. Without understanding it, we will have great difficulty appropriating our new identity and freedom from the bondage of sin.

This truth seems too good to be true. Our experience shouts the exact opposite: that our "old man" is very much alive. It seems that Paul's statements are not dealing with reality. Consequently, at this point many Christians use mental gymnastics to try to explain away (for lack of understanding) the plain teaching of Scripture. They say that the "old man" in the believer may have been "crucified" in some sense of the word, but he is not actually, literally dead. To them this old person is still very much in existence. They would typically respond, "If you think my old man died, you haven't spent enough time around me. He is alive and well."

Not surprisingly, many of us, therefore, seem to be trying to put the old man—the root source of our sin—to death. Whether we are trying to live by faith *as though* the old man is dead, or by some method of spiritual discipline, we simply cannot put to death or crucify the old man. Why? Because he is *already* dead (and buried). We cannot do what God has already done for us. Notice the past tense: "our old man *was crucified* with Him." Just as our Lord was decisively and actually crucified, so our old man was decisively and actually crucified because of our spiritual union with Him in His death.

Here is what three godly, respected scholars and teachers have said about the death of our old man.

John Murray:

> The term "crucified" is that of being crucified with Christ and therefore indicates that the old man has been put to death just as decisively as Christ died upon the accursed tree. To suppose that the old man has been crucified and still lives or has been raised again from this death is to contradict the obvious force of the import of crucifixion. And to interject the idea that crucifixion is a slow death and therefore to be conceived of as a process by which the old man is progressively mortified until he is finally put to death is to go flatly counter to Paul's terms. . . . Exegetically speaking, it is no easier to think of the old man as in the process of crucifixion or mortification than it is of the resurrected Lord as being still in the process of crucifixion. . . . The old man is the unregenerate man; the new man is the regenerate man created in Christ Jesus unto good works. It is no more feasible to call a believer a new man and an old man, than it is to call him a regenerate man and an unregenerate. And neither is it warranted to speak of the believer as having in him the old man and the new man. This kind of terminology is without warrant and it is but another method of doing prejudice to the doctrine which Paul was so jealous to establish when he said, "Our old man has been crucified." [2]

W. H. Griffith Thomas (italics mine):

The "old man" *ceased to exist* at our regeneration, when it was "put off." We are never exhorted to "put off" the old man. An exhortation to "put off" the old man would be tantamount to an exhortation to become regenerate. [3,4]

D. Martyn Lloyd-Jones:

Understand that the "old man" is not there. The only way to stop living as if he were still there is to realize he is not there. That is the New Testament method of teaching sanctification. The whole trouble with us, says the New Testament, is that we do not realize what we are, that we still go on thinking we are the old man, and go on trying to do things to the old man. That has been done; the old man was crucified with Christ. He is non-existent; he is no longer there. . . . If we but saw this as we should, we would really begin to live as Christians in this world. [5]

Something at the very core of the believer's being has been dramatically and permanently changed. We are new creations with new identities, sharing in the resurrection life of Jesus Christ. The "old man" has been replaced by the "new man." We now have a new identity at the deepest level. We are no longer essentially sinners, but new men, new creations in Christ.

In *Birthright,* David Needham tells the story of a "wicked boy" that illustrates the inadequacy of a gospel that fails to fully acknowledge the death of the old man.

I've been a wicked boy. Recently I was caught in the act of one of my many thieveries, and was brought before the judge. Looking down on me, he pronounced a huge fine which I could never pay. But then the judge paused, stepped down, and stood beside me. "I will pay your debt," he said. "In fact, I will take you into my own family to live in my home and eat at my table. You will be trained by a private tutor." So the judge took me home. The tutor has taught me how to wash my hands and hold a fork and how to be polite and clean up my language. . . ."[6]

The illustration is portraying us as the wicked boy before new birth and God as the judge who paid the debt of our wickedness at the cross, but then made us part of His family. The boy is no doubt benefited by all this, but there was no intrinsic change within him. As Needham goes on to say, "But I am still me! You see, the illustration simply doesn't go far enough."

Forgiving and adopting the boy and then placing him into a positive atmosphere was totally inadequate. New birth in Christ involves a profound change of inner being. It is not simply a change of status or environment and behavior; it is a change that takes place deep within our hearts. We were "by nature children of wrath" (Ephesians 2:3). But now we are children of God—children who are by spiritual birth trans-formed persons.

How did God bring about this radical change within us? God's method was to put to death that "wicked boy" (the unregenerate us), to execute us at the cross with Christ. In other words, He did not "recycle" the old person. He put to death the old man, buried him, and then *replaced* him with the *new man* in union with Christ in His resurrection. We have undergone the marvelous exchange!

Understanding and applying the truth of the literal death of old man is essential for two reasons. First, as Romans 6:1–14 (and especially 6:6) reveals, it is the basis of our deliverance from the bondage of sin. If we ignore or misinterpret this crucial truth, we are going to be significantly missing a foundational and vital ingredient in our ability to live in the marvelous freedom God has provided every believer in Christ. (Galatians 2:20, Colossians 3:3,9,10, and 2 Corinthians 5:14 all state the same truth.)

Second, it is essential because without the literal death (and burial) of our old man, we would not be *resurrected new men, new creations*. And without being new men in Christ, we are unchanged at the core of our beings; we would be the same persons with the same old identity.

But what about the genuine believer who is forgiven and has the Holy Spirit living within him? His old man has been crucified with Christ and he is actually a new person—but he may not understand that this has been accomplished at the moment of new birth. This Christian, if he is earnest about living a committed life, will have a strong tendency to put much of his focus and energy on trying to crucify the non-existent "old man." He will tend to be fighting the wrong enemy. Along with this misguided struggle, his perspective will tend toward a performance-based acceptance, not seeing that he is essentially a new man, a new creation in Christ, unconditionally loved and accepted by God *in Christ.* Some will even go further and view themselves primarily as unworthy sinners before a holy God, developing a "beat on yourself theology" for being such miserable sinners, viewing Romans 7:15–25 as the normal Christian life. God's way of deliverance in Romans 6 is thus tragically neglected.

It may help here to remember the butterfly. Once, it existed only as a caterpillar. But now it has changed, and it cannot go

back to being a caterpillar. It is truly and fully a new creation—a lovely butterfly! So it is with us. We are new creations
in Christ—certainly not a fully matured new creation, but a
new creation—with a new identity.

2. The Body of Sin Rendered Ineffective

The second and subsequent result of being united with Christ
is *"that our body of sin might be done away with."* What does
that mean?

It is essential that we understand the difference between the
"body of sin" and the "old man." What is said of the "old
man"—that he is dead—is not said of the "body of sin," which
still exists in the believer. To equate the old man and the body
of sin can seriously weaken our ability to lay hold of our spiritual freedom in Christ. This was certainly true in my case.

We have just identified the "old man" as the unregenerate
person we were in Adam. In contrast, the "body" here refers to
our physical body. This is clear from other verses within the
context. However, "body of sin" cannot be translated "the sinful body," for there is no basis in Scripture for the notion that
the body is innately sinful. Rather, the "body of sin" means the
body is an *instrument* or *vehicle* of sin.

In Romans 5–8, Paul refers to sin that is still present in the
Christian, using the word "sin" forty-one times as a noun. He
elaborates on the term by describing it as "sin which indwells
me" (7:17,20) and "the law of sin" (7:23,25; 8:2). There he uses
the term "sin" as a *power* that is still within us, not merely an
attitude or action. Here in verse 6:6 it is being used in this way,
as the power of sin.

In the next part of the verse, the "body of sin" is said to be

41

"done away with"—an unfortunate translation that suggests annihilation. The Greek word is often used to mean *to render inoperative or invalid, to make something ineffective* by removing its power of control. Our old man is no more; he has been put to death. Indwelling sin works through the instrumentality of our bodies; but sin's authority has been broken because of the death of the old man in Christ's death. We have "died to sin."

You might ask: what difference does it make if the "old man" is actually dead? Sin still indwells us as believers and remains a powerful force with which we must contend. Why insist on calling it "indwelling sin" or "the power of sin" instead of the "old man"? *This question strikes at the heart of the issue of identity.* Before the believer came to Christ in saving faith, the "old man" in Adam—under the total domination of sin's power—was who we really were. This was our old identity. After we came to Christ, the new man, the new creation in Him, having been set free from sin's reign, is now who we truly have become. This is, therefore, our new identity.

If the "old man" was still within us as believers, could we at the same time experience the freedom from this control of sin referred to in verses 6 and 7? Absolutely not! This freedom is impossible as long as the original *root source* of our sin, the unregenerate old man, still is alive and well within us. That old part of ourselves had to be put to death in Christ's death and then be raised in newness of life in Christ's resurrection before we could have deliverance from the bondage of the still existent power of indwelling sin.

In other words, that old man, with the old identity, had to be replaced with the new man and his new identity. Indwelling sin has been stripped of its original source of authority in us because of our union with Christ. Indwelling sin is a principle or power which aggressively wages war within us; but it is not the old unregenerate man and therefore is not our true identity any longer. It is essential that we make this distinction.

What practical difference then does it make if you understand your true identity, your essential being? First, as we saw in Chapter 2, when you truly grasp who you are in Christ you will be able to more fully experience God's unconditional acceptance and love toward you. You will no longer depend on your performance to meet your need for acceptance. Second, when you understand who you truly are, a new creation in Christ, you will naturally want to live in accordance with your new identity. Third, when you do sin, you will recognize that you are acting against your true identity. Fourth, you will not find yourself trying to war against yourself—by crucifying the old man—as if *you* were the enemy. Finally, when you stand on the truth that you are a new person in Christ whose life is united with Christ's life, you have assurance of victory over the power of sin. You will recognize that you do not have to act contrary to who you truly are.

3. No Longer Slaves to Sin

The third and final consequence of our spiritual union with Christ is that we are no longer in bondage to sin: *"that we should no longer be slaves to sin; for he who has died is freed from sin"* (Romans 6:6c,7). Our union with Christ in His death is the basis for God's proclaiming our emancipation from slavery to sin! We do not have to behave as many former slaves did after the Civil War, choosing to remain with their old masters. We can live as ones who have been freed from bondage to the rule of sin!

Summary Paraphrase of Verses 6–7

We know this, that our old, unregenerate man, inherited from Adam, our old identity, has been crucified on the cross with Christ. God crucified Him so that our bodies, as vehicles of sin, might be rendered ineffective and powerless as an instrument of sin, so that sin now no longer dominates us. God has done this so that we would no longer be slaves to sin, that we would no longer have to sin—because our old man, who had no choice but to sin, is dead. We are not fighting a civil war, old man versus new man. The root source of sin and enslavement within our deep inner being is gone. As new creations in Christ, we have been set free from the control of sin!

PART THREE

COUNTING ON
THE EXCHANGE

CHAPTER FOUR

DEAD TO SIN AND ALIVE TO GOD

"Now if we have died with Christ, we believe that we shall also live with Him, knowing that Christ, having been raised from the dead, is never to die again; death no longer is master over Him. For the death that He died, He died to sin, once for all; but the life that He lives, He lives to God. Even so consider yourselves to be dead to sin, but alive to God in Christ Jesus." ROMANS 6:8–11

How do you as a believer overcome the power of sin on a daily basis? God's provision for you could be likened to a barge that once sank to the bottom of New York Harbor. Lying on the bottom, the barge became mired in the muck. Its owners brought in huge floating cranes, but they could not dislodge the sunken barge. A tugboat captain, however, had an idea. He directed divers to attach cables from several boats to the barge below. Then, at low tide, all of the slack in the lines was taken up, making the cable lines taut. As the tide came in and the water level rose, the cables strained to pull up the barge. The tide kept coming in, the water continued to rise, and gradually the barge lifted off the bottom and was free. Observers who did not know the secret of the incoming tide would have thought that the tugboats had done all the work. But their success was mainly due to the awesome power of the Atlantic Ocean tide.

If we as believers rely on our own efforts—our own resources—to overcome the power of sin, our lives will be as embedded as that barge in the muck of futility and defeat. But like the mighty Atlantic, the Son of God has lifted us up and set us free from the power of sin through our union with Him in His death and resurrection. As we count upon this fact, we will experience genuine spiritual freedom.

Union with Christ

In verses 8–10, the emphasis shifts from our having *died* with Christ (vv. 2–7) to our *living* with Him in His resurrection life. Verse 8 emphasizes the certainty of our living with Christ, because we have died with Him: "*Now if [since] we have died with Christ, we believe that we shall also live with Him.*" Because of our spiritual union with the Lord Jesus, when He died, we also died. When He arose, we also arose and we now live with Him.

The key to understanding verses 9 and 10 is in seeing the believer in union with Christ. What happened to Him also happened to us; what is true of Him is true of us. Verse 9 explains: "*Knowing that Christ, having been raised from the dead, is never to die again; death is no longer master over Him.*" Christ's resurrection from the dead is the guarantee that He conquered the power of death. His death can never be repeated and is irreversible. Death has no more authority or mastery over Him. Therefore, our spiritual union with Him in His resurrection assures us that death has been vanquished for us once for all. Now and forever we live with Him because we are in Him.

The same line of reasoning continues in verse 10: *"For the death that He died, He died to sin once for all."* In His death and resurrection Christ "died" to death—that is, He experienced death once for all of us and now death no longer has any domination over Him. Nor does it have any domination over us, who are in Him. Likewise, in His death (and consequent resurrection), Christ "died" to sin—that is, He experienced sin once for all of us and now sin no longer has any mastery over Him, or over us who are in Him.

The last part of verse 10 states: *"but the life that He lives, He lives to God."* This refers to His resurrected life. Jesus dealt fully with sin in His death on the cross. With that once-for-all experience with sin behind Him, He now "lives to God." He is now fully and marvelously alive to the Father!

Because of our spiritual union with Christ, we now live with Him. The death that He died to sin once for all, we also died. And the life He now lives to God, we also live. This is exactly what the summary statement of verse 11 states: *"Even so consider yourselves to be dead to sin, but alive to God in Christ Jesus."*

Dead to Sin and Alive to God

We shall now concentrate on the summary statement of verse 11. It begins with the transitional phrase *"even so"* which refers to what has just been said about Christ, especially in verse 10:

because we are vitally joined to Him, we are therefore given this exhortation to *appropriate* to ourselves what happened to Him.

The exhortation to us is to *"consider"* (NASB) or *"count"* (NIV) or *"reckon"* (KJV) ourselves to be *"dead to sin, but alive to God in Christ Jesus."* The Greek New Testament uses the word *logizomai,* which has two meanings: first, literally, to simply count, number or calculate something. It was a book-keeping term. Second, metaphorically, to acknowledge or count as true what is already true.

Therefore, the *very basis* for living the Christian life, to experiencing power over indwelling sin and an "active" relationship with God, is to count on what God has already done for us by placing us into union with Christ in His death and resurrection.

Dead to Sin

The first reality that we are to count on is that we are *dead to sin.* As I noted in Chapter 1, it is critical to understand both what this does and does not mean.

- It does not mean that we as believers are immune to sin or temptation, or that sin as a force in us has been eradicated, or that we will never sin again. The Scriptures never teach sinless perfection.
- It does not mean that we *should* die to sin. God is not commanding us to die to sin. He is telling us that we have *already* died to it. God cannot command us to do what He has already done for us.
- It does not mean that we are dead to sin as long as we are in the process of gaining mastery over it. That

would make the statement refer to something experiential, and it does not do that. It refers to a past event.

- It does not mean that reckoning ourselves dead to sin makes us dead to sin. That is backwards. What Paul is saying is that because we *have* died to sin, we are to count on it—this being an already accomplished fact.

What does it mean that we are dead to sin? It means that we have been freed from sin's control. Our old man, inherited from Adam, was enslaved to sin. He had no choice but to sin. But when our old man was crucified with Christ (Romans 6:6) and we were raised a new man in Him (Ephesians 4:24), our enslavement to sin was broken. Our new man is free from the control of sin. Being dead to sin means that we are now able to *not sin*. In other words, we do not *have* to sin anymore.

Let me emphasize a very significant point here. The engine which drives this Romans 6 train is the *truth* that we have died to sin. As a result, we *are* dead to sin. If I reckon myself dead to sin, I am dead to sin. If I do not reckon myself to be dead to sin, I am still dead to sin. The critical fact is what God says is true: I *am* dead to sin. My failure to count on it does not nullify that fact. What is crucial, therefore, is that I know for certain that I am dead to sin. Once I know that for sure—once I have chosen to accept what God says is true—then reckoning or counting on it is not a struggle.

Counting on what we know to be true is natural. I am an American. If I travel overseas and then return to the U.S., I do not worry about whether I am American enough to get back into the country. I *am* an American. Without thought, I count on that fact to enable me to get back into the country.

Likewise, I *am* dead to sin. If I know that for certain, it is simply natural for me to count on that as I go through my day. When temptation arises, I know that sin has no authority over me. By counting on what is already true, I can ignore sin's attempt to trick me into submitting to its control. As Watchman Nee stated, "When we know, then we reckon spontaneously."

Kent Hughes, in his book on Romans, gives us a practical example of what it means to be dead to sin.

> When as a young teenager Stuart Briscoe was drafted into the Royal Marines during the Korean War, he came under the control of a particularly imposing regimental sergeant major who strode around the barracks leaving a train of tough men quaking in their boots. Briscoe did not realize how dominant this man had become in his life until the day he was released from the Marines. Clutching his papers in one hand, he was luxuriating in his newfound freedom to the extent of putting the other hand in his pocket, slouching a little, and whistling—sins so heinous that if they had been observed by the sergeant major, they would have landed him in big trouble! Then Briscoe saw him striding toward him. On an impulse he sprang into the posture of a Marine until he realized that he had died to him. He was not dead, and neither was the sergeant major, but as far as the sergeant major's domination of his life was concerned, it was all a matter of history. So Briscoe did some reckoning, decided not to yield to the man's tyranny, and demonstrated that fact by refusing to swing his arms high and march as if on parade and keep his back at ramrod stiffness. Instead he presented his feet, hands, and back to his newfound freedom as a *former* Marine—and the sergeant major could not do a thing about it.[1]

There are, of course, limitations to the illustration. Our old man, enslaved to sin, actually *did* die with Christ. He wasn't simply discharged. However, what is true is that, like the former Marine, we no longer have to yield to what used to have power over us. Rather, we must keep counting on what is true: that we died to sin. As sin generates those tempting, deceiving, or accusing thoughts to our mind, we must keep counting on the fact that we are dead to sin's control.

Alive to God

The second reality we are to count on is that we are *"alive to God in Christ Jesus."* In verse 5 we have seen our aliveness to God: *". . . certainly we shall be also in the likeness of His resurrection."* And again in verse 8: *". . . we believe that we shall also live with Him."*

Experiencing new birth and participating with Christ in His resurrection life have transferred us from a condition of being dead to God and alive to sin, to being alive to God and dead to sin. Our "aliveness" to God means that we are now in a personal, living relationship with God through Jesus Christ. What marvelous freedom and privilege we now have with our God! And we are to "count on" this already established vital union with Him no matter what the circumstances may be.

Believers often struggle with thinking that they have been separated from their union with God. They have sinned too much and God seems now far off. But once we have become a new creation in Christ, we are always in union with Him. Nothing can nullify that relationship.

What is needed when we have sinned as believers is to confess our sins, count on our already existing union with Christ,

1 Jn. 1:9

53

and then, as we shall see in our next chapter, *"present ourselves to God as those alive from the dead, and our members as instruments of righteousness to God"* (Romans 6:13).

Being alive to God also means that we can trust moment-by-moment that He is alive to us—or, more specifically, in us. That is, we can trust that the triune God, who lives within us, is sufficient to meet every situation and need that may arise in our lives. Such a faith walk trusts not in our ability to live the Christian life, but in Christ's ongoing ability to manifest His life through us as we consciously depend upon Him.[2]

Conclusion

The key to making our already accomplished death to sin and aliveness to God a reality in our everyday experience is to count on these facts to be true. Ruth Graham, in a *Christianity Today* feature entitled, "Remember Your Position," illustrated what the heart of this chapter conveys.

> The local sheriff had decided to tighten the requirements for his deputies. Each man had to qualify on the firing range, and the distance had been extended from 15 to 25 yards. So the deputies gathered to try their hand at hitting the target at the increased distance. Each man had 18 seconds to get off 12 shots.
>
> The best shot in the area is also a personal friend, who, the day before the trials, had been fitted with his first pair of tri-focal glasses. When his time came to shoot, he drew a bead on the target. Suddenly, as he told me later, "I began to perspire. And when I perspire my glasses fog up. There I was with a bead drawn on the target and all I could see was fog. Then I remembered what our old navy instructor had taught us: "If (for some reason) you ever lose sight of the target," he said, "just remember your position."

"So," my friend said, "I just held my position and pulled the trigger as fast as I could. By then I had less than 18 seconds, but I got off all 12 shots. When I took off my glasses and wiped them, I had hit the bull's eye every time."

There are times when we, for some reason, lose sight of our target—which is to glorify our Lord. The world is too much with us. Tears blur our vision. Unexplained tragedy raises questions that cannot be answered and shakes our faith to its foundation. Then we must remember our position, for the Christian's position is "in Christ." As if we were a tired or hurt child, he will gather both us and our load. Though we may not see the target through the fog, if we just "remember our position," we won't miss.[3]

We must remember the literalness of our present position with Christ in His death, burial and resurrection and by faith choose to count on what God has done for us in Him—even when circumstances, feelings, and human reasoning shout the opposite to us. Often we must choose *against* what seems to be the reality (based on our thoughts and feelings) and choose *for* what seems to be the unreality (God's Word). By doing so, the "sunken barge" of our lives, embedded in the dominance and defeat of sin, is gloriously lifted up and made free as we *count* on what God has done for us in Christ's death and resurrection!

In the next chapter we will see more fully how to *appropriate* these foundational truths in our daily lives.

Summary Paraphrase of Verses 8–11

Since we share in Christ's death, we also share in His resurrected life. Death has no domination over His resurrected life. Likewise, it has no domination over us. Sin has no domination over His resurrected life. Likewise, it has none over us. Just as Jesus died to sin, we died to sin. Just as He lives now to God, we live to God. Our responsibility is to simply count on these things to be true. They are true, whether we believe them or not. We are dead to sin. Because of that, when sin tempts us, we can respond, "I'm dead to that. It has no authority over me." We are alive to God. Because of that, we can say in all circumstances, "Christ's life in me is completely sufficient for this situation. I can rest in His sufficiency."

PART FOUR

PRESENTING YOURSELF TO GOD IN VIEW OF THE EXCHANGE

CHAPTER FIVE

"Just Do It!"

"Therefore do not let sin reign in your mortal body that you should obey its lusts, and do not go on presenting the members of your body to sin as instruments of unrighteousness; but present yourselves to God as those alive from the dead, and your members as instruments of righteousness to God. For sin shall not be master over you; for you are not under law, but under grace." ROMANS 6:12–14

Someone recently gave me a beautiful sweatshirt. On it was an ancient Christian symbol of the Trinity and the words, *"Just be it!"*—a takeoff, of course, on the popular slogan, *"Just do it!"*

Which comes first? As we have seen in Romans 6:1–11, we must "be it" before we can "do it." It is not what we *do* by way of performance that sets us free from the bondage of sin. On the contrary, spiritual freedom is available to us as believers because of what God has made us to *be* through our union with Him.

The sequence, therefore, is *"be it"* followed by *"do it."* The "be it" side of our spiritual freedom in Christ has been presented in Romans 6:1–11. In verses 12–14 we have the "do it" side. The apostle now explains how to *apply* our death to sin in everyday experience. It is important to understand that what God exhorts us to do in verses 12–14 will not work in our lives unless we first know and count upon who we already are in Christ (vv. 1–11).

In this chapter I am going to depart from my usual procedure of expounding almost exclusively from the Romans 6 text. Instead, I am taking a more topical approach by including a few passages which will help clarify what verses 12–14 imply.

An exhortation to do something comes in verse 12: "*Therefore do not let sin reign in your mortal body that you should obey its lusts . . .*" God has already dethroned sin from its reign in our lives. We must now "do it" in the sense that we are not to allow sin to influence us to "obey its lusts."

Indwelling Sin Versus Sinning

At this point it is critical that we define specifically what verse 12 means by *sin*. We must make a clear distinction between sin as a verb (action) and sin as a noun. In Romans 5–8, the pivotal section in Scripture on deliverance from the power of sin, the Greek noun translated "sin" (*hamartia*) is used forty-one times; the verb form (*hamartano*), four times. The noun form is often used in the sense of a governing power, principle, or law in this section of Romans, and this use of the noun form appears here in verse 12 (as well as 5:21; 6:14, 17; 7:11, 14, 17, 20, 23, 25; and 8:2).

In Romans 7:14–25, for instance, we see the term *sin* being used as a governing power or principle. There the Apostle

Paul describes himself at one stage in his life as a believer in great conflict with indwelling sin, experiencing protracted defeat. But he makes a clear distinction between "I" and "sin which indwells me" (vv. 17,20).

Notice, however, Paul is not trivializing his responsibility for having sinned when he says, "*so now, no longer am I the one doing it, but sin which indwells me*" (v. 17). On the contrary, as the rest of the passage reveals, he experiences hatred toward his actions and remorse for having submitted to the power of sin within himself.

Paul acknowledges that two entities within him are in conflict:

- "I"—Paul, the new man in Christ, who deeply desires to do the will of God, and
- "sin"—a power or principle within Paul that is the source of his defeat

note in review

It is crucial to note here that "sin" is decidedly not "I"; there is a *definite differentiation* made between "I" and "sin." Romans 7:23–25 makes an even stronger distinction between "I," the new man in Christ, and the power or principle of sin within. In verse 23 Paul refers to indwelling sin as a "different law (or principle)," which he designates as "the law of sin." This law of sin is in conflict with the "law of [Paul's] mind," the mind of the new man in Christ.

As we progress through Romans 6:12–14, we will see that making this distinction between the new man in Christ and the power of sin is crucial, both to our understanding of how the power of sin works within the believer, and to our recognition and appropriation of who we are in Christ. Only when we keep this distinction clear can we consistently experience the spiritual freedom God has already provided for us in Christ.

How Do We Prevent Sin From Reigning?

The second exhortation to "do" something is found in verse 13. The reign of sin has been broken in the believer's life. How do we appropriate this deliverance? Paul now begins to unfold the answer to this question:

> . . . and do not go on presenting the members of your body to sin, as instruments of unrighteousness; but present yourselves to God, as those alive from the dead, and your members as instruments of righteousness to God.

We are not to present, or offer, to sin the various parts of our body: our eyes, ears, tongues, hands, feet, etc. But what controls all of these members of the body? It is our *mind!* Therefore, the key to preventing sin from reigning in our lives centers on our *thought life!*

According to Romans 7:23,25 a war is being waged against "the law of the *mind*" (the mind of the new man in Christ) by "the law of sin" (indwelling sin). Romans 12:1–2 also emphasizes that our minds are the key to this spiritual warfare:

> I urge you, therefore, brethren, by the mercies of God, to present your bodies a living and holy sacrifice, acceptable to God, which is your spiritual service of worship. And do not be conformed to this world, but be transformed by the *renewing of your mind*, that you may prove what the will of God is, that which is good and acceptable and perfect. (italics mine)

Romans 12:1–2 begins similarly to Romans 6:13 and then points to the *mind* as being foundational to the presentation of our bodies to God. Second Corinthians 10:5 is even more specific when it states that we are to take "every *thought* captive to the obedience of Christ" (italics mine) as we overcome spiritual strongholds. Larry Christenson has well said, "Every spiritual battle is won or lost at the threshold of the mind."

The Modus Operandi of Indwelling Sin

How does the power of sin operate? Having combined the above passages with verses 12 and 13 of Romans 6, we see a pattern: when the opportunity presents itself, indwelling sin generates a temptation, an accusation or a deception in the form of a *thought.*

Many of us have alarm systems in our homes. If you are coming home and the alarm has been set, you know that a signal will come on when you enter your home. You will have a few seconds to disarm the system. Otherwise, the alarm will sound.

When thoughts that originate from indwelling sin enter into our minds, we must promptly disarm them, just as we would a home alarm system. We cannot stop the thoughts from coming and they may come with great frequency, but we do not have to accept and respond to them. It is essential that we learn to discern the source of our thoughts. To combat sin we need to know the difference between thoughts from the Scriptures, the Holy Spirit, or the new man, in contrast to those from indwelling sin. Only then can we reject the latter.

The way indwelling sin typically operates is to produce a thought very subtly in the form of a first-person personal pronoun (I, me, my, myself, mine). An example of such a thought is "I am such a loser." If we do not make the distinction between "I" (the new man in Christ) and "sin which dwells in me," and we receive the wrong thought as if it were coming from the real us, we have opened ourselves to sinning in our thought lives. Before we know it, we have agreed with the thought and have said to ourselves, "Yes, that is true. I *am* a loser." In doing so, we have taken responsibility for the thought and have sinned in our minds. We have also denied who we are in our union with Christ—new creatures who have a new identity and a new enablement.

Other common, first-person thoughts that indwelling sin might generate include:

"I just can't endure this one more second."

"I've had all that I can stand and I'm going to tell him so."

"I can handle myself. I don't need God to help me."

"No one has ever loved me. No one will *ever* love me."

"I hate myself. I literally despise myself."

"I never, never do anything right."[1]

When we accept these kinds of thoughts, not only have we sinned in our thought lives, but inevitably we find ourselves *choosing to act* in accordance with these thoughts. We end up sinning in our behavior. We have *"presented the members of our body to sin, as instruments of unrighteousness."*

Releasing the Life of Christ Within Us

If we focus only on the negative part of Romans 6:13 (as we have just done), we will live in defeat. We will be frustrated in our attempts to resist temptation. To experience the spiritual freedom that God has provided for us, we must also apply the positive part of verse 13. We must *"present ourselves to God as those alive from the dead, and our members as instruments of righteousness to God."* yield

At this point many are saying, "I've tried counting myself to be dead to sin and alive to God on the basis of my participation in the death, burial and resurrection of Christ. But sin and its lusts still reign to a significant extent in my life. All of this may work for others, but it is not working for me! I feel much more like the opposite of verse eleven—alive to sin and dead to God. I am defeated and disillusioned. What's wrong?!"

The reason for this all-too-familiar lament is often that we are reacting to our circumstances with our feelings rather than with our faith in the Word of God. But beyond that common problem is the one we now encounter in the passage. It centers on the word *present* (verse 13).

Many people can get all excited about these truths and the new identity in Christ. They believe that they have found the key to the overcoming Christian life. But unless they present themselves and their members to God on the basis of Romans 6:3–11, all of this will never be truly life changing for them. They will not *experience* the reality of spiritual union with Christ but rather will end up disillusioned. They will be unable to break the will cycle of defeat in their lives.

However, we must be warned at this point that the appeal to present ourselves and our members to God is commonly made to believers without reference to our already established union with Christ in His death, burial and resurrection. As a result, too many sincere believers tragically suffer unnecessary and continuing defeat.

So what does it mean specifically to present ourselves? "Present" (*paristemi* in the Greek) means to put a person or a thing at the disposal of another. This exhortation is directed to *"those alive from the dead"*—to those who are already partakers with Christ in His death and consequent resurrection. Negatively we are *"not to go on presenting the members of our body"*—our eyes, ears, hands, feet, tongues, etc.—to our old master, sin, to be *"instruments of unrighteousness."* Positively, we are to *"present [ourselves] to God as those alive from the dead, and [our] members as instruments of righteousness to God."*

First, God Himself is the focal point of this presentation. It is critical to emphasize that in our placing ourselves at the disposal of God and presenting our members to Him, our offering must be to a Person—the Person of God in Christ. At the very heart of this act is a *personal, intimate, deep love relationship* with Him. Simply knowing and counting on the truth of our union with Christ in His death, burial and resurrection and presenting ourselves to Him—without this personal, intimate relationship being at the center of this process—will eventually cause all of this to become a perfunctory, sterile and even legalistic experience. *The focus must preeminently be on God.*

Second, "present" is a word of whole-hearted *commitment* in which the entire personality is involved. The use of "present" in Romans 12:1 confirms this: *"I urge you therefore, brethren, by the mercies of God, to present your bodies as a liv-*

ing and holy sacrifice, acceptable to God, which is your spiritual service of worship." This presentation, or yielding, of ourselves as a living sacrifice refers to the burnt offering of the Old Testament sacrificial system. The entire offering, except the blood, was burned and totally consumed, symbolizing the offering of the totality of the believer's being. In this presentation, to the best of our knowledge, we are acknowledging that we are not our own. Rather, we are relinquishing the authority of our lives to Christ.

The initial putting yourself and your members at the disposal of God is followed by a continuing process. Ruth Paxson gives an example of how this presentation develops into a process.

– A man and woman through mutual faith and love yield themselves to each other in marriage. Neither of them knows then all that is involved in this surrender to each other. The wife knew that her time must be given to making the home but she had not realized how little opportunity would be left for the things she had formerly done. She rebels and uses time for things which necessitates neglect of home duties. Misunderstanding and estrangement follow. Or the husband knew that money would be required to care for his wife and supply the needs of the home but he did not know what extravagant tastes she had nor what a poor manager she was. So he has to use money he wished to spend on his business or his own pleasure. He rebels and trouble ensues. What do this husband and wife do? Do they remarry each time a misunderstanding or disagreement comes? Even the idea is absurd. If they are sensible and truly love each other they will acknowledge that there was more in the marriage vows than they realized at the time; each will recognize that all, not a part, was given in the mutual surrender and each will be willing to yield unselfishly and gladly to whatever makes for their mutual interest and welfare. Happy and harmonious married life demands not only an initial act of yielding but a continuous attitude of yielding.[2]

So it is in the Christian walk. The believer has become married to Jesus Christ (Romans 7:6) and he responds by the *process* of yieldedness to the One with whom he was united initially.

Third, "present" is also a word of *faith, of dependence.* Keeping in mind the analogy of marriage, let us focus on the marriage ceremony itself. In Ephesians 5 we see the bride or wife representing the believer and the groom or husband representing Christ. In the marriage ceremony, the bride presents or places herself at the disposal of the groom. She is to submit to his leadership (verses 22–24) and respect him (verse 33). This is not only an attitude and act of commitment, but it also is one of *faith and dependence.* There are few things that require dependence more than a bride placing herself at the disposal of the groom. For the rest of her life she is dependent on him to love her (v 25), to lead her (v 29) and cherish her (v 29). This would also imply providing for her and protecting her.

As we present ourselves to the Lord, we do so with deep gratitude for His awesome mercies to us (Romans 12:1). We are also acknowledging that we don't have in our own human resources what it takes to live this life we have been called to. We are, in dependence, placing ourselves in the hands of God to do with us whatever He chooses and give us what is needed to live this humanly impossible Christian life.[3]

Presenting ourselves to God, we must guard against the

human tendency to rely upon our own efforts, resources and abilities. Rather, we must resolutely choose to *depend on Christ,* who in all of His resurrection life now lives within us and enables us to be "instruments of righteousness." We must rely upon Him, not ourselves, if we hope to win the spiritual battle taking place within us.

In summary, presenting ourselves and our members to God has at least three elements: focusing on a personal God, commitment to Him and dependence upon Him.

Concluding Statement (Verse 14)

This magnificent section, the gospel to Christians (verses 6:1–14), concludes with a summary statement which consists of two parts, each introduced by the word "for." The first is, *"For sin shall not be master over you . . ."* This is not a command, nor an exhortation as in verses 12 and 13. It is a declaration, a statement of God's purpose and provision for us. The mastery of sin has been broken because of our spiritual union with Christ in His death, burial and resurrection. New creations no longer have to submit to the reign of sin because we are now under the reign of Christ. We need not let sin have any mastery in our lives, for that would be to act inconsistently with what God has done for us in Christ.

The second "for" explains the first statement of verse 14. The reason sin shall not master us is *"for [we] are not under law, but under grace."* This phrase has two meanings. The first use of this phrase concerns our *justification*—God's righteousness imputed or credited to us. God has declared us righteous—declared us blameless from the guilt and condemnation of our sin. The principle by which we are justified is *by grace through faith.* As chapters 1–5 of Romans so clearly explain, all our attempts to gain God's acceptance by our own efforts are futile. The average man on the street imagines salvation to be like a pair of scales. He reasons that if his good works outweigh his bad works, God will accept him in that ultimate day of judgment. And even if somehow the good works are outweighed by the bad works to some degree, God will accept him anyway because He is too merciful a God to condemn him to hell. Only when we place our faith in the grace of God (provided in Christ's substitutionary death on the cross) are we no longer "under law, but under grace."

The second meaning of the phrase relates to our *sanctification*—righteousness imparted to us by God. Christ's perfectly righteous life has been imparted within us, which in turn leads to a life of growth in holiness. The principle is the same as with the first usage: *by grace through faith.* Sanctification occurs not through our own self-effort, but by God's grace through our moment-by-moment faith in Christ within us.

Once we have been saved by grace through faith, we still have a strong tendency to live contrary to what God has done for us. Even as believers we easily find ourselves living "under law" and not "under grace." We may try to attain sanctification or spirituality by good works. If we rely upon our own human resources—our effort, abilities, or personality—to fulfill the will of God, we are *functioning* "under law" and not "under grace." We are back under the domination of sin.

Believers often reason that they can become acceptable or "spiritual" through good works: "If I read my Bible and pray each day, if I faithfully participate in church, partake of communion, give financially, consistently share my faith with non-believers, live a life characterized by care for others and

70

obedience toward God—then I will be acceptable to Him as a believer."

By no means am I minimizing any of the above practices. They are essential to a vital and growing walk with God, but they do not at all gain acceptability with Him. We are *already* unconditionally loved and accepted by God. And that love and acceptance has its foundation not only in Christ's substitutionary death, but also in our spiritual union with Him in His death and resurrection. We consequently *experience* the enabling power of the Holy Spirit to live this humanly impossible life as we *present* ourselves to God.

If we walk by *faith*, depending totally upon Christ with whom we are in spiritual union, we will *function* "under grace" and not "under law." Then we will experience freedom from the control of sin.[5]

How can living by grace instead of law work in our daily lives? Let's look at a couple of examples. Say you have been hurt by a family member or work associate. Living under law, this would be a likely response:

> This person really bugs me! I don't know why God doesn't change this person. But I've got to hold my temper and try to forget about it. God requires me to forgive 70 times 7 times, so I guess I have no choice but to ignore what is happening to me. I should act like a loving person in order to be a good Christian.

To the same situation, by the power of the Holy Spirit, you could respond this way:

> I'm angry about what this person has done to me. This hurts! I feel humiliated, misunderstood, and rejected. But I choose to welcome this situation as an opportunity to let Christ express

His life through me. I receive this negative situation as a blessing in disguise. Since I am a new person in Christ, I am a forgiving person . . . even when I don't feel like it. Not to forgive would be inconsistent with my true identity. After I forgive, I'm free to ask God to cause me to see this person with His eyes and to discover the hurt inside this person that is causing the negative behavior. I'm going to look for an opportunity to bless this person and will ask the Lord when I might need to confront this person in love about this negative behavior.

What about temptation to yield to an immoral sexual opportunity? A law-based response might be:

God says I shouldn't do this. Even though I want to do it, I must say no to my desires and grit my teeth and obey God. Holiness demands that I resist this temptation. I have to say no to this situation or God might punish me.

In contrast, a response based on grace, as one who is initially struggling with the temptation, could be:

Even though I feel like I want to sin, I choose to agree with God that I have been crucified with Christ and have died to sin. Therefore, these thoughts and feelings are not coming from who I essentially am, but from the power of indwelling sin. I am a righteous, holy child of God who is secure and significant and who really does not want nor need to yield to this temptation. Since I know who I am in Christ, I'm free to say yes to myself. I choose to believe that God will meet my emotional needs for intimacy as I trust Him.

God intends for us to live as Jesus did, not by following a set of rules, but by a moment-by-moment relationship of total dependence upon the Spirit within us. In doing so, we need to remind ourselves to live consistently with what God has

already done for us in Christ. We must learn to appropriate
what it means to *"just be it"* in order to *"just do it"*!

Summary Paraphrase of Verses 12–14

*Since these things are true, don't let the power of sin con-
tinue to control your life. You are free from it! Instead of
making yourself available to the power of sin, to do what it
wants through you, make yourself available to God, to do
what He desires to do through you. You do this by: focusing
on an intimate love relationship with God, putting your
entire life at His disposal, allowing Him to renew your
mind through His Word, and fully depending on Him. This
is all possible because we no longer live under a law-based
system, in which we try as hard as we can to live up to
God's standards. Instead, we live under grace, in which we
can simply trust Him moment by moment to be our
enablement. We are in spiritual union with God, who in
and through us is all that we need.*

Summary Paraphrase of Romans 6:1–14

How should we respond to this tremendous grace of God? Should we just go on sinning, so that God has an opportunity to show more and more of His grace? Absolutely not! That is preposterous! If that is your response, you have completely missed the truth of what God did to you and in you at the cross. You have died to sin. It no longer has control over you. How could you possibly still live that old, miserable way? You have already been freed from it.

Don't you realize that you have been placed into spiritual union with Christ? That is how God brought about your death to sin. The old you was under the domination of sin. But when Christ died on the cross, you died with Him. When He was buried, you were buried with Him. When He was resurrected, you were resurrected with Him. This means that whereas once you were partakers of Adam and the sin and death that he brought, now you are partakers of Christ's resurrected life. That is your new identity. You are perfectly accepted in that new identity. And you are able to live victoriously through His resurrected life in you.

We know this, that our old, unregenerate man, inherited from Adam, our old identity, has been crucified on the cross with Christ. God crucified him so that our bodies might be rendered ineffective and powerless as an instrument of sin, so that sin now no longer dominates us. God has done this so that we would no longer be slaves to sin, that we would no longer have to sin—because our old man, who had no choice but to sin, is dead. We are not fighting a civil war, old man versus new man. The source of sin within our deep inner being is gone. As new creations in Christ, we have been set free from the control of sin!

Since we share in Christ's death, we also share in His resurrected life. Death has no authority over His resurrected life. Likewise, it has no authority over us. Sin has no authority over His resurrected life. Likewise, it has none over us. Just as Jesus died to sin, we died to sin. Just as He lives now to God, we live to God. Our responsibility is to simply count on these things to be true. They are true, whether we believe them or not. We are dead to sin. Because of that, when indwelling sin tempts us, we can respond, "I'm dead to that. It has no authority over me." We are alive to God. Because of that, we can say in all circumstances, "Christ's life in me is completely sufficient for this situation. I can rest in His sufficiency."

Since these things are true, don't let the power of sin continue to control your life. You are free from it! Instead of making yourself available to the power of sin, to do what it wants through you, make yourself available to God, to do what He desires to do through you. You do this by: focusing on an intimate love relationship with God, putting your entire life at His disposal, allowing Him to renew your mind through His Word, and depending on Him fully to manifest His life through you. This is all possible because we no longer live under a law-based system, in which we try as hard as we can to live up to God's standards. Instead, we live under grace, in which we can simply trust Him moment by moment to live His life through us. We are in spiritual union with God, who in and through us is all that we need.

⚛

LIVING IN DEPENDENCE
UPON GOD

I N THE BEGINNING, God created man for life in the Spirit. That is, He designed man for a life of total dependency upon God, who is Life. That life was made possible through a permanent union of God's Spirit with man's spirit. As Paul says, "The one who joins himself to the Lord is one spirit with Him" (1 Corinthians 6:17). David Needham describes God's original design in his book *Birthright:*

> God's purpose in creating us is so that we, through a dependent relationship with our God, could receive and display the very life of God—the glory of God.[1]

The Source of Jesus' Life

Let's take a look at the earthly life of Jesus in this regard. We can be sure that the life of our Lord, the only perfect Man, demonstrated God's design for humanity.

If ever there was a person who would seem to have the ability to make life work on His own, it was Jesus. He was, after all, the Christ. He had no need of any help to live the Christian life. He *was* God the Son!

As we look especially at the Gospel of John, however, what we see is not Jesus' ability to live independently. Just the opposite. We see His total dependence upon God the Father. According to Jesus, the life that people saw in Him was actually Him relying on life coming directly from the Father. Everything about His life originated with the Father; nothing originated with Him.

> "Truly, truly, I say to you, the Son can do nothing of Himself unless it is something He sees the Father doing . . ." (John 5:19)

> ". . . the living Father sent Me, and I live because of the Father . . ." (John 6:57)

> "I do nothing on my own initiative, but I speak these things as the Father taught Me." (John 8:28)

> ". . . believe the works, that you may know and understand that the Father is in Me, and I in the Father." (John 10:38)

> "He who has seen Me has seen the Father. . . . Do you not believe that I am in My Father, and the Father is in Me? The words that I say to you I do not speak on My own initiative, but the Father abiding in Me does His works. Believe Me that I am in the Father, and the Father in Me . . ." (John 14:9–11)

Jesus' life was the very picture of dependence, a moment-by-moment receiving of the life of the Father within Him. There is no hint in these verses of Jesus on His own trying to live perfectly, so that He could qualify as our perfect sacrifice. There is no hint of Jesus trying independently, on His own, to do anything at all. Rather, the Lord pictures Himself as a vessel; the source of His life is the Father. His part was one of total dependence upon the life of the Father.

The Source of Our Life

We must ask, if Jesus described His own life as that of receiving the life of the Father, what does He say about our lives? *Exactly the same thing!* There is no difference between how Jesus lived His life on earth and how He wants us to live our lives.

> "Just as the living Father sent Me and I live because of the Father, so the one who feeds on Me will live because of Me." (John 6:57 NIV)

> "If any man is thirsty, let him come to Me and drink. He who believes in Me, as the Scripture said, 'From his innermost being shall flow rivers of living water.'" But this He spoke of the Spirit, whom those who believed in Him were to receive . . . (John 7:37–39)

> "In that day you shall know that I am in My Father, and you in Me, and I in you." (John 14:20)

> "Abide in Me, and I in you. As the branch cannot bear fruit of itself, unless it abides in the vine, so neither can you, unless you abide in Me. I am the vine, you are the branches; he who abides in Me, and I in

him, he bears much fruit; for apart from Me you can do nothing." (John 15:4,5)

Only God has life within Himself. Yet while on earth, even God the Son lived not with Himself as the source of life, but with the Father as His source of life. Jesus is the perfect human. In His life we see the pattern He describes for our lives: that of total dependence on God to be life within us, a total absence of depending on our ability to find, create, or manage life ourselves.

Separated from the Source

Let's go back in time further than two thousand years—back to the beginning. As we have seen, man was never intended to "make it" on his own. Man was created to be a recipient of a constant flow of life directly from God, the life that Jesus, the perfect Man, manifested on earth.

But man sinned against God. And when he sinned, much more happened than a simple act of disobedience. Instead of being a recipient of God's life, man chose to seek life on his own, to be independent, to find life within himself and through his own abilities. As Needham explains:

[Adam and Eve] became independent creatures, cut off from the life of God. Cut off from His mind, His perfection, His purity. Life for them . . . had to be found *within* themselves. . . . They were on their own. . . . They lost dependent life from God. They were now "dead in trespasses and sins." If they were to find meaning in their existence . . . they had to do it on their own. "Flesh," that is, everything mortal about them, became very important. Of course it was important—*it was all they had.* Brains, emotions, senses, creativity, imagination, bodies. Life was here, in the flesh. It was nowhere else.[2]

What is flesh? Paul uses the term repeatedly in Romans and Galatians. James Stewart explains in *A Man in Christ* that "flesh" is "human nature in its frailty and weakness and in need of help. It is man apart from God." As Needham says, "Man was never made for life in the flesh." But that is where he found himself after he sinned in the Garden: independent of God. Since Adam, all of humanity has been born into this condition (Ephesians 2:1–3).

A New Option

As believers, we have been given a new source of Life within us, the same source Jesus had. We have been given a new heart, a new spirit, created in the likeness of Christ, and we have been given the Holy Spirit, joined in union with our spirit. God has taken up permanent residence within us.

Unlike unbelievers, who have no choice but to live in the flesh, we can at any moment either live by the flesh or by the Spirit. That is, our lives can either be energized by the life of the Holy Spirit within us, or by our self-effort, trying to make life work on our own. Paul makes that choice clear in his letters to the early churches:

> . . . who do not walk according to the flesh, but according to the Spirit. For those who are according to the flesh set their minds on the things of the flesh, but those who are according to the Spirit, the things of the Spirit. (Romans 8:4b-5)

> But I say, walk by the Spirit, and you will not carry out the desire of the flesh. For the flesh sets its desire against the Spirit, and the Spirit against the flesh; for these are in opposition to one another . . . (Galatians 5:16–17)

Stated simply, our capacity to live in dependence upon God (by the Spirit) stands in opposition to our capacity to live in dependence upon ourselves (by the flesh).

What is grace living? It is living in dependence on the Spirit, not in dependence upon our own resources to make life work, or our ability to remember and live by rules.

Grace does not simply mean that God has forgiven us of our sins. It does not simply mean that God steps in to help out when we mess up trying to live the Christian life. Grace means that God has Himself done everything necessary to enable us to receive, experience, and manifest life—His life. That includes forgiveness, but encompasses so much more.

The entire gospel of Christ is a gospel of grace, from first to last. It is not a gospel of us doing our best on our own and God's grace filling in when we fall short. Grace means that we live in total dependence on God, moment by moment. That is how God designed us to live. It is not God's contingency plan because man sinned. Man was always designed to live dependently on God. His sin was trying to live independently. The gospel is the good news of God's restoration of our lives to God's original design: dependence upon Him.

OLD MAN VS. NEW MAN

CAN THE REGENERATE MAN be both an "old man" and a "new man"? Is he partly an "old man" and partly a "new man" at the same time? Is he acting from the "old man" when he sins and from the "new man" when he does what is right? Is there a struggle between two "men" within the same person? The answer to these questions has profound implications for the believer.

The term "old man" (freely translated "old self" in many versions) is found in Romans 6:6, Colossians 3:9, and Ephesians 4:22. The term "new man" (freely translated "new self") is found in Colossians 3:10 and Ephesians 4:24.

> . . . knowing this, that our *old self [man]* was crucified with Him, that our body of sin might be done away with, that we should no longer be slaves to sin . . . (Romans 6:6)

Do not lie to one another, since you laid aside the *old self [man]* with its evil practices, and have put on the *new self [man]* who is being renewed to a true knowledge according to the image of the One who created him . . . (Colossians 3:9–10)

But you did not learn Christ in this way, if indeed you have heard Him and have been taught in Him, just as truth is in Jesus, that, in reference to your former manner of life, you lay aside the *old self [man]*, which is being corrupted in accordance with the lusts of deceit, and that you be renewed in the spirit of your mind, and put on the *new self [man]*, which in the likeness of God has been created in righteousness and holiness of the truth. (Ephesians 4:20–24)

Romans 6:6 states with great clarity that we who are in union with Christ are no longer the persons we were before regeneration. Our old unregenerate man was crucified with Christ. Colossians 3:9–10 confirms that believers have already (in the past) "put off" the old man and "put on" the new man.

The only passage which seems to contradict the perspective of Romans 6:6 and Colossians 3:9–10 is Ephesians 4:22–24. There, most standard versions translate the putting off and the putting on as *imperatives* or *commands,* implying that the believer has coexisting within him both an old man (which he needs to put off) and a new man (which he needs to put on). But in the Greek text there are no imperatives or commands, only infinitives (*apothesthai* and *endusasthai*), which mean "to put off" and "to put on."[1]

Although it is not grammatically incorrect to translate these infinitives as commands, as most of the standard versions do, it is also correct to view them as "explanatory infinitives"; that is, they would explain what is stated in the preceding context (vv. 17–21).[2] Ephesian believers must no longer live as the Gentiles do since they were taught, with regard to their former way of life, to put off the old man and to put on the new man who has been created to be like God in true righteousness and holiness. The New International Version appropriately translates the infinitives in verses 22–24 as "explanatory infinitives":

> You, however, did not come to know Christ in that way. Surely you heard of him and were taught in him in accordance with the truth that is in Jesus. You were taught, with regard to your former way of life, to put off your old self, which is being corrupted by its deceitful desires; to be made new in the attitude of your minds; and to put on the new self, created to be like God in true righteousness and holiness.

However, even if we accept the translation of the infinitives as commands, we need to be aware that Paul's emphasis was clearly on the believer's *behavior*. He then would be using the infinitives in the sense that his readers were to put off the *old ways* of the old man and to put on the *new ways* of the new man. David Needham has explained it well:

> It was as though Paul saw a believer standing before two wardrobes; one contained the clothing (lifestyle) of an unregenerate person. "Take them off," Paul urged. "They don't fit, they're out of style, totally unbecoming of who you are, and, if that were not enough, they don't belong to you." The other contained the clothing (lifestyle) of a regenerate person. "They're yours!" Paul exclaimed, "Wear them. Don't worry, they'll fit!"[4]

We see the same emphasis on behavior in Romans 13:14: "But *put on* the Lord Jesus Christ and make no provision for the flesh in regard to its lusts." This command was written to

Christians, to those who had already put on Christ in regeneration. They were to "put on," "clothe" themselves with Christ in the sense of saying, "Christ is yours: wear Him."

Taking into account Romans 6:6, Colossians 3:9–10, and Ephesians 4:22–24—as well as the entire teaching of the New Testament—believers have been radically transformed from what they were before conversion. We are no longer the persons we once were. We are not at the same time both our old selves (old man) and our new selves (new man), but are new persons in our union with Christ. Paul puts it another way in 2 Corinthians 5:17: "Therefore, if anyone is in Christ, he is a new creature; the old things passed away; behold, new things have come." As John Murray stated: "It is no more feasible to call the believer a new man and an old man, than it is to call him a regenerate man and an unregenerate."

Indeed, we are no longer the old unregenerate man who was enslaved to sin; we are now the new regenerate man who has been freed from the domination of sin and who participates in the resurrection life of Christ. We have become new creations, new persons at the very core of our beings. As we view ourselves in this way, acting in dependence upon Christ, our lives will be revolutionized.

Thoughts on the New Man

I will conclude Appendix II with comments from various writers on the believer's true identity.

A. W. Tozer:

"Is justification from past offenses all that distinguishes a Christian from a sinner? Can a man become a believer in

Christ and be no better than he was before? To be a sinner confessed and consciously lost *is* necessary to the act of receiving salvation . . . but here is the truth which has been overlooked in our day. A *sinner cannot enter the kingdom of God.* . . . The penitent sinner meets Christ and after that *he is a sinner no more.* The power of the gospel changes him . . . and makes him a new creation . . . for the work of Christ sweeps away both his good and his evil and turns him into another man . . . it also includes an actual change in the life of the individual . . . a transformation as deep as the roots of his human life. If it does not go that deep, it does not go deep enough." [5]

John MacArthur:

"If you are a Christian, it's a serious misunderstanding to think of yourself as having both an old and new nature. We do not have a dual personality! Assuming the dual nature of the believer could easily lead one to excuse all kinds of sins by blaming them on the old nature. . . . The popular theological concept of the old man and the new man fighting each other is not biblically accurate. According to the Apostle Paul, the old man has been put off, having been replaced by the new man. The believer is a new creation—not a perfected creation—but still a new creation. . . . The old man has ceased to exist. Salvation brings about a radical change in the nature of the believer." [6]

Charles Swindoll:

"Why should sin gain the mastery over us? Who says we cannot help but yield to it? How unbiblical! . . . many Christians put the old man in a case and greet him every morning and cater to him every day of their lives. We live as though our 'old man' is alive, even though we are dead to him. He has no right to be in our conscious thinking. . . . Our *identity* was changed.

. . . When we came to Christ we were placed into Him as His death became ours, His 'awakening' to new life became our 'awakening,' His powerful walk became our powerful walk. . . . He lives in me and I live in Him. And in this identification with Him, His power becomes mine. His very life becomes my life, guaranteeing that His victory over sin is mine to claim. I no longer need to live as a slave to sin." [7]

D. Martyn Lloyd-Jones:

"The greatest truth we can ever be told is that our old self has gone. I can deal with [the body of sin] only as I realize that my *old self has gone and I have a new self.* This is a most striking and amazing truth. The problem of [the body of sin] becomes much easier once I realize that my old self has gone. My old self, that self that I was in Adam, was an utter slave to sin. That self has gone; I have a new self, I am a new man. Is not that a marvelous thing to be able to say? I am not doing this or that, it is this sin that remains in my members that does so. . . . This is the most liberating thing you have ever heard!" [8]

Freedom From The Law

ROMANS 6:14 DECLARES: *"For sin shall not be master over you, for you are not under law, but under grace."* Since this topic is not developed by Paul in Romans 6:1–14 (but rather in Romans 7), it is not within the scope of this book to elaborate on what it means to not be *"under law, but under grace."* But since this truth is so crucial to our spiritual freedom in Christ, this section of the appendix is devoted to it.

Just as the believer's participation in Christ's death, burial and resurrection has freed us from the bondage of sin (Romans 6), so also this union frees us from the bondage of the law (Romans 7).

Romans 7:1–6 is the apostle's explanation in Romans of what

it means for us to be no longer *"under law, but under grace."* Verse 1 of chapter 7 sets forth the general principle: *death is the only way for us to end our relationship with the law.* Verses 2 and 3 give an illustration of this general principle: a wife is bound by law to her husband as long as he lives, but if he dies she is freed from the law concerning her husband and can marry another man. The point of the illustration is that death is the only thing that frees us from the jurisdiction of the law.

The general principle (v.1) and the illustration of that principle (vv. 2–3)—*that death is the only way for God to end our relationship with the law or with being "under law"*—is applied in verses 4–6. In verse 4 we see that the believer's death to the law or law-principle was effected *"through the body of Christ"* (which refers to His death on the cross). Because of our Savior's substitutionary death which satisfied the just demands of the law, and because of our spiritual union with Christ in His death (and consequent resurrection), *"we were made to die to the Law."* As believers, we are like the widow who was freed from the old relationship with the first husband when he died; now we have been *"joined to another"* husband, namely Christ, *"who was raised from the dead."* The purpose of this new union with the risen Christ is *"that we might bear fruit for God."*

In 7:5 we see that our old unregenerate life was characterized by *"sinful passions, which were aroused by the Law"* (cf. Romans 7:7–12). These sinful passions *"were at work in the members of our body to bear fruit for death."*

Paul summarizes his application in verse 6: *"But now we have been released from the Law, having died to that by which we were bound."* Consequently, believers are enabled to live *"so that we serve in newness of the Spirit and not in oldness of the letter."*

So what does it mean that we are no longer *"under law, but under grace"* (6:14) or that *"we were made to die to the Law"* (7:4) or that *"we have been released from the Law, having died to that by which we were bound"* (7:6)? Obviously, it does not mean that we have been given a license to sin now that we are not under the bondage of law-principle, but under grace (6:15 ff.). It also does not mean that the law has ceased to be a revelation of God's character and truth.

Then what *does* it mean to be dead to the law and therefore released from its bondage? First, our relationship with the law before regeneration resulted only in *condemnation* by revealing the true nature of our sin and failure. But now that very condemnation has been removed from us by Christ who satisfied by His death on the cross the righteous demands of the law. Second, our relationship with the law before regeneration resulted in *increased slavery* to sin because our sinful passions were actually aroused by the law (7:5,8). Even as a believer, Paul, in Romans 7:15–25, describes his personal experience of agonizing struggle and miserable defeat, trying to keep the law in his own efforts. But now our death to the law has released us from its deceptive bondage (7:4,6,11).

But even more foundationally, to be dead to the law and therefore released from its bondage means that *we are not under an achieving system (law), but under a receiving system (grace) for acceptance with God.* Law-principle or law-keeping says: do, perform, and then you will be accepted by God. Grace says: your acceptance has already been provided in Christ apart from your efforts or performance.

Contrasting Law and Grace

	LAW	GRACE
Type of System . . .	Achieving system	Receiving system
Says . . .	Do	Done
Emphasizes what . . .	Man does	God does
Lives out of the . . .	Flesh (self-life)	Spirit (Christ-life)
Draws on . . .	Man's resources	God's resources
Deals with . . .	External standards	Inner heart attitude
Primary focus . . .	Ought-to's, musts, shoulds, have-to's	Want to's
Creates . . .	Bondage, duty	Freedom
Lives life from the . . .	Outside in	Inside out
Declares . . .	"Do, in order to be"	"You are, therefore, do"
Produces . . .	Defeat, guilt, condemnation	Victory, security, acceptance
Operating principle . . .	Try harder, work	Receive, trust, rest

Endnotes

CHAPTER 1

1. Bob Smith, *From Guilt to Glory* (Palo Alto, Calif.: Discovery Publishing, 1978), 13.
2. John MacArthur, Jr., *The MacArthur New Testament Commentary: Romans 1–8* (Chicago: Moody Press, 1991), 307.
3. David Needham, *Birthright* (Portland, Ore.: Multnomah Press, 1979), 60.
4. James M. Boice, *Romans, Volume 2: The Reign of Grace, Romans 5:1–8:39* (Grand Rapids: Baker Book House), 650.
5. Neil Anderson, *A Way of Escape* (Eugene, Ore.: Harvest House Publishers, 1994), 122–123.
6. Boice, *Romans, Volume 2: The Reign of Grace*, 670.
7. Larry Christenson, *The Renewed Mind* (Minneapolis: Bethany Fellowship, 1974), 41.

CHAPTER 2

1. Maxwell Maltz, *Psycho-Cybernetics* (North Hollywood, Calif.: Wilshire Book Company, 1964), 28.
2. For additional examples of Spirit baptism see 1 Corinthians 12:13 and Acts 1:5. Also, in 1 Corinthians 10:2 "baptized" is used in the sense of identification with Moses' leadership, not water baptism.

3. Kenneth S. Wuest, *Word Studies in the Greek New Testament: Volume 1* (Grand Rapids: Wm. B. Eerdmans Publishing Co., 1973), 96–97.

4. Implications of becoming partakers of Christ's resurrection are discussed in Chapters 4 and 5 and Appendix I.

5. In addition to the vine and the branches, other examples in Scripture of our union with Christ are: The Lord's Supper (1 Corinthians 11:24,25); the temple and the chief cornerstone (Ephesians 2:20–22); the head and the members of the body (Ephesians 1:22–23 and 4:15–16); and the husband and wife in marriage (Ephesians 5:32).

6. John Murray, *Redemption Accomplished and Applied* (Grand Rapids: Wm. B. Eerdmans Publishing Co., 1955), 170.

7. Arthur W. Pink, *Spiritual Union and Communion* (Grand Rapids: Baker Book House, 1971), 7.

8. Boice, *Romans, Volume 2: The Reign of Grace*, 795.

9. We are raised presently in spiritual union with Him, participating in His resurrection life. In the future our metamorphosis will be complete as we take on resurrection bodies.

CHAPTER 3

1. Charles R. Swindoll, *The Grace Awakening* (Dallas: Word Publishing, 1990), 104–105.

2. John Murray, *Principles of Conduct* (Grand Rapids: Wm. B. Eerdmans Publishing Co., 1957), 212–213.

3. W.H. Griffith Thomas, *St. Paul's Epistle to the Romans* (Grand Rapids: Wm. B. Eerdmans Publishing Co., 1946), 168.

4. For a more thorough treatment of the new man replacing the old man, see Appendix II.

5. D. Martyn Lloyd-Jones, *Romans, The New Man:*

An Exposition of Chapter 6 (Grand Rapids: Zondervan, 1973), 68.
6. Needham, *Birthright*, 53.

CHAPTER 4

1. R. Kent Hughes, *Righteousness from Heaven* (Wheaton, Ill.: Crossway Books, 1991), 127.
2. For a more detailed explanation of living in dependence upon Christ, see Chapter 5 and Appendix I.
3. Ruth Graham, "Remember Your Position," *Christianity Today*.

CHAPTER 5

1. Taken from *Defeating Sin*, an audio tape series by Bill and Anabel Gillham.
2. Ruth Paxson, *Life on the Highest Plane* (New York: Fleming H. Revell, 1928), 53–54.
3. For a more detailed explanation of living in dependence on Christ, see Appendix I.
4. For further detail on living by grace, not law, see Appendix III.

APPENDIX I

1. Needham, *Birthright*, 23.
2. Ibid., 23–24.

APPENDIX II

1. These infinitives are in the present tense, implying a process. The new man in Christ has been made actually and genuinely new, but he has not yet been made totally new. As Anthony Hoekema states: "The newness of the

new self (man) is not static but dynamic, needing continual renewal, growth, and transformation." He still strug-
gles against sin and on occasion yields to sin. But he is no
longer enslaved to sin.

2. Cf. Anthony Hoekema, "The Reformed Perspective" in
   Five Views on Sanctification (Grand Rapids: Zondervan
   Publishers, 1987), pp. 80–81.

3. David Needham, *Alive for the First Time* (Sisters, Ore.:
   Multnomah Books, 1995), 276.

4. Murray, *Principles of Conduct*, 218.

5. A.W. Tozer, *The Divine Conquest* (Camp Hill, Pa.:
   Christian Publications, 1992), 36-37.

6. John MacArthur in *Masterpiece*, March/April 1990,
   18-21.

7. Swindoll, *The Grace Awakening*, 109, 115, 117.

8. Lloyd-Jones, *Romans, The New Man*, 83.

Operation 220 Ministries
2001 W. Plano Pkway, Suite 3800
Plano, Texas 75075
(972) 941-4442
admin@operation220.org
www.operation220.org

Christ Centered
Biblical Counseling,
Teaching and Training

DICK FLATEN was an extraordinary man of God who left behind a legacy of integrity and faithfulness. Exhibiting a contagious devotion to and personal communion with Christ, his life's example and his exposition of the Scriptures reached countless souls for the kingdom of God.

Born in 1930 in Illinois, Dick surrendered his life to Jesus Christ as his Lord and Savior while attending the University of California at Berkley. He became involved in the same college ministry through which he heard the gospel, at First Presbyterian Church. Dick completed his BA in architecture, then began preparing for vocational ministry, earning a Bachelor of Divinity from Bob Jones University.

Dick joined the staff of Campus Crusade for Christ at Texas A&M University, during which time he met and married his wife Ann. Together they served on the Campus Crusade staff at the University of Texas at Austin. From 1960 to 1968, Dick pastored Branham Lane Baptist Church in San Jose, California. He received a Masters of Theology from Dallas Theological Seminary in 1969, after which he was invited to be the founding pastor of a church in Austin, Texas based on sound biblical exposition. He pastored Grace Covenant Church for 19 years. The church grew into a dynamic ministry which helped birth other Bible churches.

In 1989, Dick and Ann moved to Dallas, Texas, where they served with the Center for Church Renewal at Fellowship Bible

Church North, teaching and leading home and church-based Bible studies. Later Dick accepted a similar position with Exchanged Life Ministries in the Dallas area. He and Ann also taught through the ministry of their church, Park Cities Presbyterian.

Dick's greatest joy in ministry was emphasizing not only the moment-by-moment supernatural resources of the living Christ, but also God's available grace to experience Christ's life. Dick's own life was an authentic testimony to the sufficiency of Christ in daily living, as in 1975 Dick was diagnosed with non-Hodgkins lymphoma, a form of cancer. During his remaining 23 years, he counted it a privilege and opportunity to glorify the Lord in his illness, becoming a living example of the reality of Paul's words to the Philippians: "For to me, to live is Christ and to die is gain."

Dick's favorite passage to study, preach, and teach was Romans 6-8, in which Paul most thoroughly establishes the biblical foundation for supernatural Christian living. Dick completed his exposition of the first part of this beloved passage two months before he went to be with the Lord. *The Marvelous Exchange* is Dick's ongoing ministry to the lives of countless more believers, proclaiming the message that Dick, given the time, would have most wanted to share in each of their homes.